The Courage
the Heart Desires

The Courage the Heart Desires

Spiritual Strength in Difficult Times

Kathleen Fischer

JOSSEY-BASS
A Wiley Imprint
www.josseybass.com

Published by Jossey-Bass
A Wiley Imprint
989 Market Street, San Francisco, CA 94103-1741   www.josseybass.com

Jossey-Bass books and products are available through most bookstores. To
contact Jossey-Bass directly call our Customer Care Department within the U.S. at
800-956-7739, outside the U.S. at 317-572-3986, or fax 317-572-4002.

Jossey-Bass also publishes its books in a variety of electronic formats. Some content
that appears in print may not be available in electronic books.

Text design by Paula Goldstein.

Library of Congress Cataloging-in-Publication Data

Fischer, Kathleen R., date.
  The courage the heart desires: spiritual strength in difficult times /
Kathleen Fischer.
     p. cm.
  Includes bibliographical references (p. 163).
  ISBN-13: 978-0-7879-7595-1 (alk. paper)
  ISBN-10: 0-7879-7595-8 (alk. paper)
  1. Fear—Religious aspects. 2. Courage—Religious aspects. I. Title.
  BL65.F4F57 2006
  241'.4—dc22   2005028346

Printed in the United States of America
FIRST EDITION
HB Printing   10 9   8   7   6   5   4   3   2   1

Contents

For Tom

Preface

In recent years, I have noticed a common theme running through my conversations with clients, family, and friends. We all yearn for inner and outer peace, yet we often experience instead a disquiet that mutes joy and hope. Anxiety about both minor and major matters troubles us. There are the personal situations that evoke fear: facing an audience, anticipating a medical diagnosis, surviving a divorce, making a major life transition, staying afloat financially, or keeping kids off alcohol and drugs. But larger fears also press us, like gravity above and beyond these everyday concerns. The events of September 11, 2001, along with the reality of global terrorism increase the perception that unnamed perils can strike at any instant.

This book grows out of my deepening realization of what a factor fear is in our lives. Our personal happiness and the future of this fragile universe may very well hinge on how we deal with it, for fear plays a much larger role in our motivations than most of us realize. It is a great destroyer of possibilities. Like a roadblock that brings traffic to a standstill, fear stands between us and the fullness of life

God envisions for creation. Gifts for music, writing, or leadership remain unexplored because we are afraid of criticism
or failure. New careers and promising relationships go
unenjoyed because the challenge of change is just too
daunting. Peace and justice remain unrealized because we
fear so much those we have labeled "the enemy" that we
spend almost no time talking to them. The fear of death,
always lurking, keeps us from ever really choosing to live.

I am convinced that the spiritual is our most important resource for moving through these fears to courage and
hope. Faith gives our efforts assurance that God is with us,
and that makes a huge difference. I write for spiritual seekers everywhere, whether or not they belong to a church or
synagogue or attend religious services. Although my own
background is Christian, I draw from many and diverse spiritual perspectives. How we encounter worldviews different
from our own constitutes a crucial aspect of peace and justice as we begin the twenty-first century. I have learned a
great deal from other religious traditions, and I want my
comments to reflect something of the richness of that
exchange. I also include research in psychology and other
disciplines that throws light on our current situation.

While struggling with anxiety, we find ourselves
drawn with admiration to the courageous among us. We
want to believe that we too can be brave in the face of fears,
whether they concern the risk of relationship or the fate of
our planet. Like fear, courage appears in small and large
guises, and I try to treat both kinds throughout this book.
Those who carry out great acts of courage rely on the daily

courage of the many, and ordinary courage in turn draws inspiration from extraordinary instances. We in the Northwest have an image from nature of this mutual exchange among those who share life's challenges. We see flocks of Canadian geese flying in formation across the sky. It looks as if the goose in the lead has the hardest job of all, battling the wind resistance. It *is* hard work. But the beating of so many wings in that V formation creates an updraft that supports the leader and actually makes that position much easier to fly. In an interdependent world, our seemingly insignificant acts of courage likewise have power to uplift others.

Because we need to understand fear's dynamic before we can deal with it wisely, my first chapter looks at fear's function, and how it can be a blessing before it becomes a burden. I then show how bringing our fears into a relationship with God helps us sort through them, heeding some and learning to let go of others. Subsequent chapters chart the spiritual passage from anxiety that paralyzes us to the courage we desire: ways to stay in the present moment, practices of meditation, prayers for frightening times, methods of nurturing hope, and paths to the love that moves us past fear. I clarify the meaning of courage and show how powerfully it circulates among us in our increasingly interconnected universe. Finally, I offer the words and lived example of spiritual mentors from many eras who teach us where genuine security lies. My goal throughout is to uncover the wealth of spiritual resources available to us as we seek to bring hope into our frightened world.

If you wish to read more about some of the topics I treat, a section of Notes and Further Reading offers suggestions for pursuing issues in greater depth. My hope is that this work will contribute to the peace, joy, and sense of adventure God desires for us all.

Chapter One

Understanding Fear

Fear is a reminder that we are creatures—fragile,
vulnerable, totally dependent on God. But fear
shouldn't dominate or control or define us.
Rather, it should submit to faith and love.

—PHILIP BERRIGAN

MYSTICS, POETS, AND LOVERS tell us that the heart
has its reasons, which the mind does not know.
They name the heart the center of emotion, the symbol for
love and hate, grief and rage, tranquility and fear. So we
speak of being heartbroken, of having a heavy or peaceful
heart. So much that truly matters happens at this deep level:
the warmth that delights us in a freshly discovered love, the
anguish that envelops us when a marriage falls apart, the
anxiety that gnaws when a friend falls ill. But sometimes we
cannot tell whether we are angry, sad, or anxious, so we fix
something to eat, have a drink, or busy ourselves by surfing
the Web. Emotions nevertheless play themselves out in
body and mind, relationships and families, work and poli-
tics. Knowing what to make of emotions, and what to do
with them, determines not only health and happiness but

1

holiness as well. Much of what happens in the spiritual life depends on directing their energy wisely.

This applies especially to feelings of fear, a primary emotion that alerts us to matters of life and death. A mother sees her toddler about to fall from a playground slide and catches him just in time. A couple out for an evening walk jump out of the path of a careening car. Fear's sudden surge of insight and energy fuels these reactions. It protects lives. But anxiety can also disrupt our sleep, render our bodies rigid, and prevent us from flying or attending a social event. Fear helps or hinders in countless ways.

The fact that we experience fear as friend and foe raises questions. Should we calm our fears, or ramp them up? How does fear fit into a healthy spirituality?

The fact that we experience fear both as aid and ordeal, as friend and foe, raises several questions. Should we calm our fears, or ramp them up? How does fear fit into a healthy spirituality? The answers rest on recognizing the great diversity that marks the human experience of fear. Like love, it comes in many shapes and sizes. A rich array of terms describes its many manifestations: *anxiety, terror, dread, panic, alarm, worry, awe, reverence.* We fear not only physical consequences of injury but also mental sinkholes and quagmires. We can imagine and try to avoid emotional as well as bodily pain. On this psychic level, fear branches out to embrace a

2

spectrum of experiences: failure, betrayal, embarrassment, disability, disapproval. Religion extends fear from this life to the next, with images of punishment and hell to enforce conformity.

Sorting through the expressions of fear lays the groundwork for deciding which to heed and which to heal. It also prepares us to see the essential role spiritual resources play in facing as well as assuaging fears. Let us begin by reflecting on fear as gift, and then move to those problematic forms that immobilize and limit us. Finally, let us consider a crucial element of any healthy spiritual life: what it means to fear God.

Fear as Gift

When a huge tsunami devastated the coastline around the Indian Ocean the day after Christmas 2004, observers noticed a striking phenomenon. Almost no bodies of animals were found among those of the thousands of people killed by the giant walls of water. In Khao Lak, Thailand, elephants started trumpeting hours before the tsunami. They began wailing an hour beforehand, and just before it struck they fled to higher ground—some breaking their chains to do so. Similar animal behavior was reported in India, Sri Lanka, and Indonesia. Alert to the vibrating ground, to the sound and scent of the sea, and to the behavior of other animals, they sensed imminent danger and made their way to higher ground. Many humans, on the other hand, missed the signs or failed to grasp their implications. Some brought their children to the beach to watch the unusual behavior of the ocean.

The word *fear* initially evokes only painful associations, like those now linked to the tsunami. We seldom list fear among the things for which we are grateful. But as the tsunami disaster makes clear, fear arrives as blessing as well as burden. Animals (from fruit flies to monkeys) know fear. It tells them to flee or find shelter. So also with human beings. Designed as a natural warning system, fear helps us recognize and respond to anticipated peril. In fact, the word itself derives from an Old English term for danger. It calls us to protect life, our own and that of others, and then to extend this protection outward to all creation.

The opening chapters of the biblical book of Genesis, in which we watch Adam and Eve being ejected from the Garden of Eden, contain an early account of human fear. Adam replies to God's voice, "I heard the sound of you in the garden, and I was afraid." By that point in the story, trusting relationships at every level have been fractured. In a world without sin and suffering, fear would presumably have no function. Life could thrive without the need to brace itself against possible threats. But the Book of Genesis depicts not only paradise unspoiled but also our current universe, Eden lost and not yet restored. Ours is a creation of lost innocence, riddled with danger, distrust, enmity, natural disasters, and therefore fear. Genesis is not the last time fear occurs in scripture; the Bible talks a lot about fear, telling us what to fear and what not to. Like the posters I recently saw on a Seattle bus, it reminds us both to "Look around. Be aware," and "Relax. Help is just a click away."

The immediacy and detail of worldwide communication today situates fear for our personal future within a broader horizon of global perils. We wonder about health, our own and our children's; we dread the consequences of environmental destruction, war and violence, epidemics, and biological and chemical terrorism. No conscious person could, or should, be entirely without fear in the face of such universal dangers. Like the flares at the site of a freeway accident, such warnings prompt us to prudence. In the past, fear has fueled many creative inventions that now enable us to avoid dangers. It will again prove to be a blessing if it leads us to change course and protect our planet's future.

Accepting Fear Rather Than Fighting It

A friend who has anxiously waited days for a doctor's decision about her breast biopsy finally learns there is nothing the matter with her. "I hope I never have to go through this again," she says as she comes out of the doctor's office. We know something of what she feels as she waits. Like her, we want to avoid feeling that way again if at all possible. It therefore puzzles us to learn that psychologists, Buddhist teachers, and other spiritual guides offer a similar recommendation regarding fear. The best way to deal with it, they say, is to allow it to simply be what it is. They use the terms *radical acceptance* or *befriending* for this nonjudgmental embrace of the body's reaction to danger. Psychologists term the ability to feel an emotion *affect tolerance*.

As with any of the emotions, denial complicates matters, dulling awareness in the same way a cataract clouds the pupil of the eye. Fear then often expresses itself as anger, a more socially acceptable emotion (especially for men). But if we convert the energy of fear to anger, we are likely to act out in destructive ways. As with experiences of referred pain, we do not realize the place that hurts is not the source of the trouble. The source lies somewhere else. Learning to face our fears with confidence that we can handle them creates a more direct and healthier path to what we want. With acceptance, there is room to recognize the information an emotion contains and then decide what we want to do about it. Listening to feelings in this way is the starting point for wise choices.

This implies that we need not be ashamed of being afraid. An Episcopal priest once told me about a retreat she made with other pastors. They were asked to step into a circle marked at various points with emotions such as anger, sadness, joy, and fear, and to stand wherever they most identified with a feeling. Almost none of them could acknowledge being afraid; it was too hard to ask for help and protection. Shame and embarrassment suggest that there is something wrong with us if we get scared. But Jesus himself knew fear, both in the Garden of Gethsemane, where he asked his disciples to stay with him, and earlier as he adhered to his own time frame for the final approach to Jerusalem, knowing his enemies awaited him there. The

With acceptance, there is room to recognize the information an emotion contains and then decide what we want to do about it.

gospels even describe the bodily manifestations of his terror in the Garden, how he began to be "distressed and agitated" and told his disciples, "I am deeply grieved, even to death; remain here, and keep awake" (Mark 14:33–34). Seeing Jesus' fear is one of the ways we know he is human, and it confirms the fact that deep and powerful emotions do not signify weakness but rather reveal the full range of the human response to life's events.

Some past forms of spirituality fed this shame by valuing mind over body, and reason over emotion. They linked feelings such as anger and fear to weakness and also to fuzzy thinking. Today we realize that body and mind are closely intertwined, designed like an intricate piece of embroidery. Neuroscience is dissolving some of the mystery around our emotional life, and its breakthroughs enable us to understand fear perhaps better than any other emotion. Science tells us that feelings do not exist in opposition to reason; in fact, we cannot think well or make decisions without their help.

The Tibetan meditation teacher Pema Chödrön emphasizes that by acknowledging an emotion and allowing ourselves to feel the energy of the moment, we cultivate compassion for ourselves. This frees us to experience what scares us in a new way. I discovered the truth of her insight while healing from a fear of dogs that stemmed from a childhood incident. When I was ten, my sister and I were sent to a neighbor's house to pick up our weekly supply of eggs. What we did not know was that the neighbor was away and her dog was about to give birth to puppies. Instead of the welcome we usually received, we found an agitated and defensive dog that badly bit my little sister before I could stop it. I half-carried my sister home, and she had to be taken to the hospital.

Feeling responsible for what had happened and shaken by the upheaval it created, I developed a distrust of dogs I had never known before. A first step in facing this fear was letting go of the judgments I leveled against myself for feeling scared, as well as for the incident that led to it in the first place. Then I needed to gradually be around dogs. Sitting alone and avoiding them only increased my discomfort and solidified my bad memories. Over the years, learning more about their wonderful qualities from those who love dogs, being with them on walking paths and in the homes of friends, and finding that they come with varied personalities has helped me move through this fear. Without knowing my history, my clients themselves contributed to this healing as they brought their dogs in to meet me, shared their deep affection for them, or came to me in grief over the loss of a beloved pet.

Whether we call it radical acceptance or befriending, allowing ourselves to feel and face our fears takes courage. It does not happen easily. In fact, it requires grace. The Psalms repeatedly express trust that God will be with us in handling fear and moving beyond danger.

> I *lift up my eyes to the hills —*
> *from where will my help come?*
> *My help comes from the Lord,*
> *who made heaven and earth.*
>
> —PSALM 121:1–2

Many of the spiritual practices suggested in later chapters lend support for this way of embracing fear and finding the courage we need.

When Fear Becomes a Problem

If fear is so valuable, why do we try to weed it out of our lives? Prolonged or misplaced fear shrinks the human capacity for joy, creativity, and freedom, making it impossible to fully realize the happiness God intends for us. Letting fear become a way of life also has negative physiological consequences. Fear sets in motion a sequence of bodily responses meant to help us escape danger. We cannot escape such responses altogether, and they sometimes serve a purpose. But if repeated or prolonged, they have serious consequences for health. As the brain centers that are crucial to fear keep registering potential danger, they set in motion a process that increases the body's stress hormones, which among other things makes the heart pump faster, quickens breathing, and reduces the ability to concentrate. This is helpful in an emergency, but if the body remains on this kind of alert, the stress takes a toll. It weakens the immune system and raises the risk of cardiovascular disease. The muscle tension created by anxiety produces headaches, insomnia, and back and neck pain. What was meant to be a life-saving resource now becomes itself a threat.

There are also more extreme forms of fear, conditions where fear has become pathological. Brain chemistry, genetic inheritance, childhood experiences, traumatic events, and current stress might all be causal factors. Think of these afflictions as the higher end of the fear spectrum, false alarms that cannot be turned off. They include severe trauma, panic attacks, and phobias. *Posttraumatic stress syndrome* is the term usually used for the psychological and physical difficulties that result from extreme trauma and stress, such as witnessing death or serious injury during war, or being sexually assaulted. The event is then relived in dreams, flashbacks, and other intrusive symptoms. A *panic attack* is a sudden bout of intense fear, marked physically by rapid heartbeat and shortness of breadth. A *phobia* refers to a specific fear, which may be of almost anything—heights, flying, strangers, public spaces, or closed spaces such as an elevator. Many people feel some mild fear of these things but continue to function normally. Severe phobias, however, can be incapacitating.

Dealing with serious forms of trauma, panic, phobia, or anxiety usually requires professional help, and sometimes medication. For many people, these kinds of fear involve great suffering and constitute a dark night of the soul. The good news is that there are many treatments available. Here too the spiritual dimension forms an important part of the healing process, as it strengthens and informs other approaches.

Most of us struggle with lesser forms of fear. Anxiety and worry gnaw at the edges of awareness, like a caterpillar munching away at leaves. In fact, ours has been called a culture of anxiety. Whereas fear is a limited emotion with a definite object, anxiety is an unfocused fear that reaches into all of life. Since human beings have the capacity not only to react to threats but to anticipate them as well, anxiety turns to what might happen in the future. Worry is the internal process of trying to figure out a way to escape from this potential threat. Worry often travels around with us, like a pebble in a shoe.

Anxiety is a painful and life-altering experience for those who endure it to any great degree. However, short of a serious anxiety disorder, we can often lessen it ourselves. Spiritual resources such as prayer and meditation offer powerful ways to better understand and reduce the impact of what frightens us. But fundamental to this weaving of spirituality into our experiences of fear is making sure that our spiritual

Spiritual resources such as prayer and meditation offer powerful ways to better understand and reduce the impact of what frightens us.

beliefs themselves are not compounding the problem. This means, among other things, looking at how we understand fear of God.

Fear of the Lord as the Beginning of Wisdom

Many of us who grew up in an established religious tradition learned to fear God because of the ever-looming threat of hellfire and damnation. Such fear of God served as a disciplinary device in home, school, and church. It instilled in believers a dread of eternal punishment and made them uneasy about getting too close to God lest they be judged and found wanting. But using fear as a primary religious motive, along with failing to produce healthy spiritual lives, intensified the difficulty many people already had with handling their other anxieties. Gradually spirituality has shifted to a greater emphasis on the love of God.

Although underscoring divine love helps offset the negative impact of a preoccupation with sin and guilt, it can also lessen the sense of wonder and mystery vital to spirituality. In its root meaning, *fear* connotes alarm and dread, but also reverence and awe. It signifies amazement before this immense and complex cosmos and the divine Mystery that creates and sustains it. The Bible, in fact, often uses the phrase "fear of the Lord" to describe a deep reverence for God. This awe-filled attentiveness keeps us attuned not only to God's presence, but also to divine transcendence.

Scripture tells us that fear of the Lord comes as grace, a divine gift. When the prophet Isaiah promises that his defeated and demoralized people will have a new messianic leader, he declares that the spirit will rest on this person. It will be

> *the spirit of counsel and might,*
> *the spirit of knowledge and the fear of the Lord.*
> —Isaiah 11:2–3

Then, contradicting much of what we may have been taught about fear of God, Isaiah asserts that this spirit-conferred fear will be a delight. What can this possibly mean? It indicates that such fear does not preclude love and intimacy, as human fear might. Rather, it is love that leads a person to hold God in awe. Joy and delight follow.

Further, the recognition of divine Wisdom that flows from reverence allows us to release the heavy burden of believing we have sole responsibility for, and control over, everything that happens in the universe. Instead, trust in the divine Presence that upholds all creation puts our fears in perspective. This is why biblical figures are offered two seemingly contradictory statements: "The fear of the Lord is the beginning of wisdom" and "Fear not, for I will be with you." They are told what to fear and what not to fear. Trust in the mystery of God is fundamental to overcoming their fears.

Trust in the divine Presence that upholds all creation puts our fears in perspective.

Consider also the conversation Job has with God while trying to wrench some meaning from his immense suffering. After Job has fully laid out his bitterness and despair, God speaks to him in stanza after stanza of astonishingly beautiful poetry. God offers Job an extended hymn to the universe, a sweeping vision of Creation. Verse upon verse name the wonders of the universe: teeming seas and shifting rhythms of light and darkness, drops of dew and wildly flapping ostrich wings, soaring hawks and horses leaping like locusts. God asks Job,

Where were you when I laid the foundation of the
earth?
Tell me, if you have understanding.
. . .
On what were its bases sunk,
or who laid its cornerstone
when the morning stars sang together
and all the heavenly beings shouted for joy?
. . .
What is the way to the place
where the light is distributed,
or where the east wind is scattered upon the earth?

—Job 38:4, 6–7, 24

Job's lesson in awe does not preclude a close personal relationship with God. Even as he acknowledges wonders he cannot fully grasp, Job experiences God's presence as the only real answer to his agonized questions about evil: "I had heard of you by the hearing of the ear, but now my eye sees you" (42:5). The Book of Job ends by affirming worship and intimacy as moments in the spiritual life, linked by an accurate understanding of fear of God.

Fear of the Lord, then, should produce not human cowering but true security, for it witnesses to a Wisdom beyond what we can immediately discern. As a central teaching of both the Bible and the Quran, this fear is not a debilitating anxiety; rather, it is a deep reverence for God that brings openness to divine guidance. When developed to its fullest extent, the fear of the Lord becomes the ideal

14

attitude of a human being before the Creator, almost synonymous with faith itself. One translation of the Quran renders "fear of the Lord" as "God-consciousness." A person who "fears the Lord" in this fullest sense remains ever aware of the divine purpose in the universe. Fulfilling God's desire then increasingly directs one's life.

Fear's many cadences culminate in this reverence and wonder before the Mystery that sustains us. We have seen how varied fear's manifestations can be, from clear and appropriate fear that helps us avoid danger to nameless anxiety that plagues our days, and to troubling phobias that seriously constrict us. Understanding the purpose of fear and the shapes it takes helps us determine what to fear and what not to fear—the topic we turn to next.

Chapter Two

Knowing What to Fear

Holistic discernment encourages us to put our
whole self—mind, body, feelings, imagination,
intuition, dreams—into the process of seeking
God's guidance.

—WILKIE AU

I N *TRAVELING MERCIES: SOME THOUGHTS ON FAITH,*
Anne Lamott writes about her son Sam's seventh birthday. Sam has accompanied her to a writing conference she
is teaching in the mountains of Idaho. While out on an
early morning walk, she and Sam catch sight of a dozen
paragliders floating down from the high mountain above
their valley. The beauty of their colorful silk parachutes—
aqua, apricot, lavender, rose, and red—framed by the
mountain and sky entrances them both. When the gliders
land, Sam rushes to talk to them, announcing that he will
be seven in two days. One of the pilots offers to take Sam up
with him in a harness on his birthday. He says he has been
taking his own son paragliding since the boy was five.

Sam thinks the offer is absolutely great, and he
beseeches his mom to let him go. Lamott, describing herself as not exactly the bravest mother in the world, finds

herself torn. Where, she wonders, is that fine line between being a responsible parent and being overly protective? She tries to decide whether it is a good idea to let a seven-year-old paraglide (even with an expert) off a mountain fifteen hundred feet high.

First Lamott sits by the river and prays to know what she should do. She turns over the alternatives, trying to think her way into an answer. When this just makes her mind feel like a ping-pong ball, she calls several friends and asks their advice. Half of them tell her to let Sam do it; the other half think she is crazy to even consider the idea. Some tell her to pray about it, so she prays some more. But she still does not know what to do. She wonders why God cannot give her a loud and clear answer to her questions.

After dinner the next night, as she is dancing to some mandolin music, a memory pops into her head out of nowhere. She recalls how, years ago, when faced with a difficult major decision, a minister taught her how to get quiet and listen to her deepest feelings. So right there on the dance floor, Lamott does just that. She thinks about how she would feel if she let Sam glide, and her heart immediately leaps into her throat. Then she thinks of how she would feel if she said no, and she is elated. So she cancels with the paraglide pilot. The next day, on Sam's birthday, a friend unexpectedly calls and offers to take him innertubing on a creek at the foot of the mountain. It is a level of risk she can handle.

Lamott's way of deciding whether to let her son go paragliding actually illustrates very well what the spiritual lexicon calls *discernment*. She lets God into her decision making when she prays for guidance. This readies her heart to notice God's presence within and all around her, and to listen deeply and attentively to the many ordinary manifestations of the holy in our thoughts and feelings, intuitions and dreams, in nature and in human relationships.

The discernment process is a way of examining our fears in prayerful reflection, noticing what lies beneath them and where they are taking us. In such discernment we learn which to heed and which to allay. The familiar refrain "'Twas grace that taught my heart to fear, and grace my fears relieved" from the spiritual "Amazing Grace" invites us to open our perceptions of danger to the divine guidance hidden within our lives and the world. We may not have time for this in a sudden moment of fear, as when pulling a burning pot from the stove, but using the discernment process for larger or more persistent anxieties gradually makes even our daily decisions more thoughtful and grounded.

The discernment process is a way of examining our fears in prayerful reflection, noticing what lies beneath them and where they are taking us.

No one pattern of discernment fits everyone. Some people meet with a spiritual director. Others pray alone or with friends. Most listen to their mind and body; gather information; and consult informally with family, friends, and community. In whatever way the process unfolds, it generally includes certain movements. We will explore them, focusing on how they help us identify the promptings of grace found within emotions such as fear.

Noticing What We Are Feeling

A friend going through chemotherapy for breast cancer finds herself raging at the nurses in the clinic where she gets her treatments: Why hadn't they told her she would have so much nausea? Who talked her into going through this chemo in the first place? Only when she pauses to ask why she is so angry does she realize how afraid she is. The fears come tumbling out: suffering, pain, disfigurement, dependency, death. Then from beneath the fear emerges a deeper layer of sadness. She just wants to weep from the pain of it all. Draining this sorrow eventually produces a resolve and surrender not possible before. She can then ask the nurses the questions that really frighten her: "Will the symptoms get worse with each treatment?" "Will I die soon anyway?" "What help is there?" Held over time in a community of friendship and prayer, sustained by their care and the rituals she creates with them, she eventually grieves her losses and becomes comfortable with not having answers to all her questions.

Being open to our feelings requires an attitude of nonjudgment. Letting a feeling just be itself means relinquishing comparison with people we might think of as braver, calmer, or bolder than we are. No longer berating ourselves for the feeling lets it flow. As this happens, larger fears break down into manageable size, just as turning on a light reveals the actual shapes that darkness has turned into monsters. Acknowledging the feeling permits us to explore and reflect on it, thereby identifying its elements. Since emotions are invariably mixed, anger or sadness may mingle with the fear, and we have to feel them to understand it. Though hard to face, each of these facets of a fear is actually easier to handle than the vague, nameless clutch in the stomach that goes unexamined. Paradoxically, becoming aware of fear simultaneously permits some release from it.

For example, am I afraid of a deeper intimacy beginning to develop in a new relationship? What exactly do I fear? Perhaps being known for who I am. Or rejection and hurt. Perhaps being controlled. Maybe the risk of hoping and being disappointed. I may have past wounds that I need to address. One man I saw in spiritual direction realized that because of the death of his father when he was ten he grew up believing it was dangerous to rely on others. They could leave you or die; it was better to be self-sufficient. So he always got out of relationships fast, before the other person could leave him and revive the pain he remembered. He was surprised to learn he still felt angry that his father had been taken from him so early in life. Working with the emotion freed him from some of his fear about entering more fully into present relationships.

The sixteenth-century Jesuit Ignatius of Loyola, often considered the master of discernment, proposed a way of knowing that integrates mind and body, thoughts and feelings, intuition and imagination—what Ignatian spirituality terms *felt knowledge*. One way to access this level of knowing is to imagine yourself carrying out in detail each alternative in a decision. Suppose you fantasize about quitting your job. How will you tell people? What do they say? How do you spend your days after you quit? As you imagine yourself living out this choice, notice what happens with your body and feelings. Now spend a few days fantasizing about keeping your job, in the same detail. This exercise reveals how much we already know on a deep, affective level about what we want and need to do.

At any moment of the day, two short questions take our emotional temperature: "*What* am I feeling?" "*Why?*"

> *At any moment of the day, two short questions take our emotional temperature: "What am I feeling?" "Why?"*

When someone comes to me for spiritual direction, I often suggest we start with a moment of centering in God's presence. In that silence, feelings of fear register in the person's shallow breathing, tight muscles, anxious thoughts. Pausing longer with the question "What is it I fear?" or "What makes me anxious?" brings nameless anxiety into focus ("I worry that I'm not doing enough for my mother. Should I be taking more time to care for her?" Or "I'm afraid my pain is never going to go away, and that I can't manage to live with it forever"). Sometimes giving this energy a name can itself generate relief and hope.

We want to get rid of fear. But *feeling* a fear frees us from it more effectively than anesthetizing it with alcohol, drugs, or busyness. The urge to flee from fear stems partly from the belief that admitting fear constitutes moral weakness, and partly from helplessness in face of it. Ignored, fear resurfaces at other times, often at night when our ability to cope is weakened by fatigue. Emotional wisdom consists of getting acquainted well enough with our fear, anger, and sadness that we know what triggers them, how they register in our body, and what will enable us to direct their energy positively. God's promptings are found within these natural guidance systems that have been given to us.

Putting Our Fear into a Faith Context

So human and universal an emotion is fear that it appears in even the most significant figures in the Bible. Jeremiah, whom God has in mind for a prophetic calling, feels totally inadequate. Mary of Nazareth is beset with confusion when an angel tells her she will bear a son to be named Emmanuel. Peter cowers around the fire after Jesus' arrest, desperately hoping not to be recognized by the servant girls. None receives instructions on how to cope with fear. All are simply promised a sheltering presence: "Do not be afraid. I will be with you." The love of God may call us to service in spite of our fears, just as it did our biblical forebears. It may also take us to a trust that grace will be there when we need it. The constant is God's faithfulness.

James A. Forbes, senior minister of Riverside Church on Manhattan's Upper West Side, learned such trust. He said that at the time of the September 11 attacks he found himself uncertain where the Spirit was leading him and what direction he should take. In his congregation were people who were grieving. Others struggled to find the courage to look for another job—or even to go outside. They came to his church asking, "Is there a word from the Lord?" They were searching for comfort and direction. Wanting to be anchored in faith and open to the Spirit, he wrote a prayer—a song, actually—and sang it every day.

> *Holy Spirit, lead me, guide me,*
> *as I move throughout this day;*
> *may your promptings deep inside me*
> *show me what to do and say.*
> *In the power of your presence,*
> *strength and courage will increase.*
> *In the wisdom of your guidance*
> *is the path that leads to peace.*

Forbes says that this prayer grounded his response to the impulses the crisis evoked in him. He realized he needed to return constantly to the Word for a fresh perspective. The Word, he believed, is both pastoral and prophetic, raising questions and answers. What can be said now? Take the Twenty-Third Psalm, which promises that "even though I walk through the darkest valley, I fear no evil." What is the valley of darkness? What does it mean to fear no evil when we are all scared? Nearly every text, he said, required application to the new reality.

Fear may signal real danger, alerting us to take action, like Forbes's increased awareness of evil following the September 11 attacks. The heart ought to tremble in such circumstances. But prayer may also strengthen us to find respite from the anxiety that gnaws endlessly and sees threats everywhere. Putting our fears in dialogue with God's word lets us heed some concerns and be relieved of others.

Staying Free

Ignatius used the word *desolation* for (among other things) fears that paralyze us and undermine freedom. *Desolation* might aptly describe the fear-based culture in which we live today. Last Christmas, messages from many friends sounded this note ("My personal life is going well, but the situation in the world weighs on me all the time, blotting out joy like an eclipse"). One friend about to fly to Europe put it this way: "I'm scared. There's a feeling that we've dropped to another level in the world—it isn't safe. It won't stop me from going, but it's like playing Russian roulette."

Many factors influence a sense of what is dangerous. For one thing, we fear what we cannot control. This is why driving seems safer than flying. Some people who are afraid to fly pull onto a freeway without a second thought, although statistics show that driving is much more dangerous than flying. Also, circumstances that threaten immediate harm grip us more strongly than those that work more slowly. An anthrax attack occurring even in another city scares us more powerfully than our own smoking, though the latter, with its delayed consequences, is a much more certain threat to our health.

The kind of freedom that accompanies discernment has the qualities we associate with inner peace. It includes the realization that there is much we cannot control. Risk is inherent in human life. In the words of August, a main character in Sue Monk Kidd's novel *The Secret Life of Bees*: "You've been halfway living your life for too long. May was saying that when it's time to die, go ahead and die, and when it's time to live, live. Don't sort-of-maybe live, but live like you're going all out, like you're not afraid."

I developed a prayer to remind me of this divine call to adventure whenever timidity begins to stifle my zest for life:

> *O God, you risked*
> *the perils of creating this universe,*
> *so fraught with the follies of freedom.*
> *Fill us with some of your daring.*
> *Lest we hold back, hobbled by caution,*
> *encourage us to imitate*
> *your own spirit of adventure.*
> *Sophia, Wisdom,*
> *Source of delight and joy,*
> *so creative and inventive,*
> *you rejoice in the world and*
> *in us, the human race.*
> *Alive in you, may we learn*
> *to experience a similar joy.*

Though we usually think of fear as painful, the experience of overcoming a fear can be pleasurable. We feel intensely alive, aware of our strength. Inherent in humans is the capacity for risk taking. It has enabled us to conquer the fear of fire, climb mountains, and reach the moon.

A crucial attitude buttresses the freedom we desire: acceptance of the fact that we will die. Suffering, loss, and death are all part of life. When we decide to play it safe, we are usually trying to avoid any loss. Death is the greatest one, but there are many little deaths (such as failure and rejection) that cause pain as well. If we let ourselves be governed by fear of death, we will never really live. As soon as we accept and make peace with it, we begin to enjoy new freedoms: to choose work that fits our gifts, to love others even though we may lose them, to work for justice in the world, to stay with friendships that are imperfect, to eat chocolates, and to laugh with the moon.

True freedom in the Spirit supports our daily struggle to cut

Those who get close to God find their notion of safety revised, their heart and mind enlarged, and their tolerance for risk given a boost.

through all the voices herding us into our prisons. Grace may move us into a place of personal insecurity, revising ideas we have held about how things ought to be. Those who get close to God find their notion of safety revised, their heart and mind enlarged, and their tolerance for risk given a boost. The story of John Newton, author of the hymn "Amazing Grace," is a case in point. As a sailor on an African slave ship, Newton nearly drowned when a violent storm tore his ship apart off the coast of Newfoundland. As he and his shipmates struggled to save the ship, stuffing leaks with bedding and clothes, Newton was amazed to find himself turning to prayer: "If this will not do, the Lord have mercy on us." He realized it "was the first desire I had breathed for mercy for the space of many years." Barely surviving this ordeal dramatically changed Newton. The rudimentary prayer that kept his spirit alive amid personal danger revealed a spark of faith. He decided to make prayer a part of his life.

Over time, Newton's previous blindness to the horrors of the slave trade lifted, and he saw the terrible cruelty he himself had inflicted on the slaves. When he became captain of his own ship, he finally turned it back to Africa and let his load of slaves go free. He gave up slave trading entirely and returned to England, where he became a vocal abolitionist.

Gathering Adequate Information

Discernment relies on outer information as well as inner. We make choices not as isolated individuals but as members of overlapping communities. One woman tried to practice such informed decision making in the spring and summer of 2004, when the issue of encampments for the homeless heated up in a Seattle suburb.

For some months, communities of up to one hundred homeless persons had pitched tents near several Seattle churches. Then they announced plans to move to neighborhoods unaccustomed to having the homeless living next door. Tent cities, as the communities are called, usually commit to limiting their stay at one site to three months. Plans to relocate Tent City 4 to the north Seattle suburb of Bothell generated an uproar among that community's residents. For months, neighbors debated issues of safety and fairness, but the tent city prevailed.

In late summer Tent City 4 geared up to move from Bothell to a parcel in Woodinville, where a pastor had extended an invitation for its residents to stay near his church. This prompted a neighbor, Paulette Bauman, to pay a visit to the Bothell camp. The mother of two young children, Paulette lives just a block from the church. "I try to base my decisions on facts, not fear, which is why I'm here," she said. She found the tents clean and well kept, and the mood quiet and peaceful. Still, she had concerns about the lack of police supervision proposed for the camp. She said that although some of her neighbors were already rallying against the tent city, she had a list of things to do before she made any decisions. It included talking with Woodinville officials and getting the perspective of school officials. "You want to help people and be kind," she believes. "But my ultimate responsibility is to my kids, and to protecting them." Arming herself with facts allowed Paulette to determine which fears were justified and which were not.

Accurate and realistic information, along with analysis and judgment, keeps fear grounded in the real. Moreover, checking things out, filling in the gaps in our knowledge, often actually reduces anxiety. In his book *Fear and Courage*, Stanley J. Rachman describes how using videotapes to prepare children about to enter the hospital for surgery eased their fears: "They show an actual child being treated in an actual hospital, and that helps a great deal."

A major obstacle to graced decision making today is the fact that U.S. newspapers and television news programs play to our fears. In *Creating Fear: News and the Construction of Crisis*, David L. Altheide, a professor in the School of Justice Studies at Arizona State University, tracks the nature and extent of use of the word *fear* in major newspapers from 1987 to 1996 and has examined ABC news coverage for several years. He finds that *fear* in stories and headlines increased substantially—often by 100 percent over that time period. It traveled across various topics, at times being associated with AIDS, children and schools, drugs, gangs, violence, and crime. After a while it became redundant to include the word, since the very mention of certain topics engenders it. Even though objective studies of risk indicate that most U.S. citizens are safer and healthier than at any time in history, surveys show that we consider our lives to be very threatened.

Fear, Altheide concludes, is a key element in the entertainment format that has shaped news reports for decades. It creates a fear-based society, influencing national and international affairs and constituting a foundation on which more fear can be built. Fear accumulates and washes onto the beaches of our experience, Altheide says, like agates that have been forged through time and pressure. But agates enrich our lives, whereas fear limits them and leaves us vulnerable to tyrants and would-be saviors.

Walking Wisely with Fear

How can we know if our response to danger is balanced?

Some people have too low a sense of caution or make it a point of pride to tempt fate. It is possible to become addicted to danger, driven by the high that comes from surmounting obstacles. A friend and I both agree that she has too low a sense of potential danger. She once left her purse in the car in full view; not surprisingly, it was stolen. She leaves windows open at night, even though her apartment is easily accessible from a stairway. This reflects too limited an appreciation of the real evil in the world. Like too much fear, too little awareness of risk can be harmful.

An even more striking example of gambling with danger comes from the story of Jim Wickwire. A high-altitude mountaineer, he was one of the first two Americans to reach the summit of the 28,250-foot K2, the world's second highest peak. In *Addicted to Danger: A Memoir*, Wickwire reflects on the fact that in spite of having a wife and five small children at home, and despite the deaths of several climbing companions, he was unable to keep his repeated promises to stop climbing. He recognized that he climbed not just for the beauty and solitude, the friendships and physical exertion, but also because of an attraction to danger. In the mountains he learned that he could overcome his fears and survive adversity. But as Wickwire reflects more deeply on his commitment to his wife and children, he uncovers another aspect of his motivation in challenging his limitations: "By facing danger I believed I could push back my own mortality." When his discernment takes place in the context of family and friends, their questions push him to look more fully at his motives.

Each day offers us countless choices, some leading to life and others paving a path to death. Fear is a gift that ultimately enhances the capacity to live with freedom and joy by alerting us to what truly endangers God's vision of creation. Real evils do threaten the greater good: widespread poverty and hunger, global warming, species extinction, torture, and murder. Fear of such actual threats shapes and directs the choices that will protect all beings on our planet.

Directing the energy of fear allows the wisdom of this emotion to unfold.

A pivotal biblical message about fear is found in Deuteronomy 30:19: "I set before you life and death. Choose life." Here God's hopes and desires for us are summed up. Directing the energy of fear allows the wisdom of this emotion to unfold. If we can hear its message, we can transform it into courage, faith, joy, and other ways of sustaining what we care about.

Four elements of discernment, or seeking to live in line with God's desires, sum up the path to knowing what to fear:

1. Notice and name my feelings of fear.
2. Bring these fears to faith and prayer.
3. Gather information and test conclusions.
4. Take action and watch for confirmation.

It would be unrealistic to think we can be entirely without fear. The paradox is that joy comes from acknowledging fear and living fully in spite of it. Accepting the fact that we are all vulnerable and in danger, we dare to choose life.

Chapter Three

Living in the Here and Now

People usually consider walking on water or in thin air
a miracle. But I think the real miracle is not to walk
either on water or in thin air, but to walk on earth.
Every day we are engaged in a miracle which
we don't even recognize.

—THICH NHAT HANH

A<small>N UNKNOWN LAY BROTHER</small>, assigned to do kitchen work in his Carmelite monastery in Paris, achieved amazing peace through a simple spiritual practice. Brother Lawrence's method consisted of cultivating at all times an awareness of the presence of God. He believed that no matter where we find ourselves, no matter what issues confront us, we should address them with consciousness of being in God's loving presence. Doing so renders all our activities sacred and puts us in continuous prayer. At the surface, Brother Lawrence dealt with the clatter and challenges of the monastery kitchen, while at a deeper level he possessed God in great tranquility.

One day, on a visit to his monastery, M. de Beaufort, an official on the staff of the Cardinal of Paris, struck up a conversation with Brother Lawrence. He was amazed at the depth of the brother's spirituality. Later, an account of their conversations was published under the title *The Practice of the Presence of God*. It became a spiritual classic, though Brother Lawrence himself remained in obscurity, quietly at work among his pots and pans until his death at the age of eighty.

The Practice of the Presence of God, which I first read during my own novitiate, introduced me to the apparently simple, but actually quite difficult, practice of staying in the here and now. Learning this gentle habit proves to be a powerful route to reducing anxiety. Over the years, I've learned that instructions on how to dwell in the moment lie at the heart of nearly every spiritual tradition.

> *Instructions on how to dwell in the moment lie at the heart of nearly every spiritual tradition.*

Buddhist teachings on mindfulness and wakeful presence tell us that this is where we can find the peace we crave. The Vietnamese monk Thich Nhat Hanh considers mindfulness the miracle by which we restore ourselves. He uses the example of a magician who cuts his body into many parts and places each part in a different region: hands in the south, arms in the east, legs in the north. Then by some miracle the magician is able to instantly call all the parts back and reassemble his body. This is what mindfulness does: it calls back our dispersed mind, restoring us to wholeness.

According to the ancient Jewish sages, being fully present in the moment enables us to find our place in the world. Consider a time when you tried to do a jigsaw puzzle. Reality is like that puzzle. Each piece has its place in the whole, and no other quite fits there. Nor can any piece stand on its own apart from the other chunks of the puzzle. Only when each is in its place does the puzzle come to life, its meaning now evident. Likewise, each person's mission is to take his or her place in life's puzzle, thereby bringing the elements of creation into harmony with one another. The Jewish sages call this *tikkun olam*, the repair of the world. The kabalistic or mystical path of Judaism contains a story of the world's creation that includes a cosmic shattering of vessels of light. We are to help heal creation's brokenness by bringing these sparks together again.

The rabbinic sayings collected in the *Pirke Avot* refer to God as *the Place*, the place where we are living at this very moment. If we stand fully in this place, the divine energy flows through all things and links us to one another and to God. The Hasidic sage Schneur Zalman taught that "the purpose of Creation is to reveal the Infinite in the details of the finite." Living with attention, one action at a time, is true meditation; God and holiness are found in the details.

In spite of its established place in so many spiritualities, staying fully in the moment looks like a rather foolhardy way to deal with danger. Can we really heal the past and safeguard the future if we focus on the here and now? Won't we simply fail to anticipate threats? This proves to be the fundamental paradox: present awareness counts for more than apprehension in the pursuit of peace. This becomes clear when exploring the graces the present moment offers.

Learning to Breathe

One of the first things you may notice about fear is that it tightens and constricts your breath. This is why learning to breathe is such a powerful antidote to anxiety of all kinds. Attention to the breath brings us back to the moment. It also furnishes the first line of approach in almost any discussion of reducing stress and fear. Hindu and Buddhist systems teach elaborate methods of working with the breath. But even simple, prayerful ways of turning to it help. Try to gradually breathe more calmly and fully, deepening your breath slowly. Then add your own version of a prayer that I developed to use with those I see in spiritual direction:

> *Breathing in, I open to the life of the Spirit;*
> *breathing out, I let go of my distress.*
> *Breathing in, I receive God's love and grace;*
> *breathing out, I release my doubts and fears.*
> *I breathe in peace, and release arguments and*
> *   turmoil.*
> *I breathe in azure skies, bird trills, and marigolds;*
> *I relinquish worries, tensions, and terrors.*

> *I breathe in bright colors and kind people; I let go*
> *of violence and hate.*
> *I breathe in music and dancing; I breathe away*
> *sirens and disaster.*
> *I rest in God, in the moment, breathing in and*
> *breathing out.*

This focus on one's breath can be done anytime and anywhere. Start with your normal breath and then gradually slow and deepen it. As you inhale, feel it filling your body with new energy. As you exhale, feel it leaving. As you breathe in and out, see it as the Spirit bringing fresh, rejuvenating energy, and releasing you from your fears and anxieties.

Attention to the breath brings us back to the moment and reduces stress and fear.

Being Grateful

While traveling in France in the spring of 2000, I fell down a step in a bus station in Avignon and broke my right ankle. My failure to be fully attentive likely contributed to the accident, since I was gazing at bus schedules instead of watching my step. The interns who staffed the emergency room in Arles, into which I eventually hobbled, gave me generous care. The young women working at our hotel were solicitous, even studying a French-English

dictionary until they could say "Good luck with your healing." However, my medical treatment left me coping with a
very large and heavy plaster cast and a set of unfamiliar
crutches. Making my way back home with these clumsy
appendages proved highly challenging.

At one point, as I was walking from the train to the
station in Paris, my physical and emotional strength
deserted me. I simply could not drag the cast and crutches
another inch. The platform was nearly empty, and there
were no wheelchairs in sight. What would I do? I wondered. Then I thought of my mother. It was May, very near
her birthday. I remembered how, following her stroke, she
had to learn to walk again. When she realized this was what
she had to do, she somehow found the inner resources to
get out of her wheelchair and, like one of the many toddlers
she had raised, take some first tentative steps. The memory
of her courage took hold of me and got me going again
along that long Paris platform. For the moment, I drew on
her memory to find my resolve and manage my fear.

Breaking my ankle changed me in several ways. I
love to walk, and until then I had taken it for granted. Other
aspects of my life absorbed my attention; walking was a
given. Then, during the months it took my ankle to heal,
I had to forgo hiking mountain trails and ocean beaches.
Even getting to work and around my neighborhood was difficult. I began to appreciate the ability to walk as I never
had before, and that awareness has remained with me,
extending to other gifts I am tempted to take for granted.
I find myself thanking God I can hear the bars of a

Beethoven symphony, and study the stars at night. A favorite prayer as I go to sleep consists of naming the blessings I can recall from my day, starting with very small ones I am likely to overlook: a great peach for lunch, a phone call from a friend, a kind greeting from a bus driver.

This practice has the added benefit of turning my mind from worries to the present goodness of my life. You might call it the power of positive thinking. It is hard to focus on gratitude for the moment and anxiety about the future at the same time. The flows of energy they produce differ. One expands the spirit, and the other tightens it. One reminds us that life is good, while the other calls up all possible threats to what one has.

Gratitude constitutes a simple but powerful path to mindfulness. A mother told me of a recent change she's noticed in her college-age son: "He's become so much more *aware* of things. And he's so grateful for the things we do for him. Before, he didn't seem to notice—or maybe he just took them for granted." Juggling parenting, work, and other commitments makes meditation and formal prayer seem out of reach. But noticing and giving thanks requires simply the practice of attention. Before I can experience gratitude for the dawn breaking in the sky or a child's infectious laughter, I must first take it in. The more present I am to the details of life—a friend's warm welcome, the smell of baking bread, the first crocus pushing through the snow— the more likely it is that a prayer of thanksgiving will rise up in me. Since such prayer takes just a moment, busyness need not crowd it out of life.

41

Uncovering Joy

A friend of mine recalled a recent conversation with her mother after the U.S. terror alert level was raised to orange. A snippet of it went like this:

MOTHER: "I just know something's going to happen."
DAUGHTER: "Something is always going to happen. When I'm at Fred Meyer shopping for groceries and the floor shakes, I think something is going to happen. We can't live if we keep thinking this way all the time."

Fear of the unknown haunts us more than any other. This is why terrorism is especially insidious, since no one knows where it will occur next. Yet a similar uncertainty characterizes all danger. The realization prompts us to be on alert at all times. As a friend puts it, "I feel as though we should all be afraid of everything, all the time, and everywhere."

Joy is available anywhere.

Even though appropriate fear guards us from harm, too much anxiety sucks the joy right out of existence. A preoccupation with life's dangers obscures the gifts offered us by a loving Creator. Perhaps it seems we must wait for joy until complete safety exists. But it never will. No, we cannot let our sorrows and suffering dominate our lives. The seeds of happiness lie scattered in and around us all the time. My husband's niece and family have a puppy that greets us with wild enthusiasm when we arrive. She seems convinced that joy is potentially available anywhere. She is right.

Thich Nhat Hanh describes a simple way to enjoy peace in the present moment. Instead of inquiring, "What is wrong?" he suggests asking, "What is not wrong? What is right?" This capacity to focus on what is healing and beautiful in the present moment constitutes the art of mindful living. There is no way to joy, he believes; rather, joy is the way.

The reverence that opens out into gratitude can pervade our lives. Without the dust of distant stars, the pebbles on the beach, the grass in the field, we would not exist. Everything deserves deep respect. But our capacity for happiness may currently be buried under a stack of worries. How can we free it? Thich Nhat Hanh suggests that one way lies in reciting Buddhist sutras or sayings. In *Touching Peace*, he offers two mindfulness verses that cut to the core of anxiety. After the longer form of each, he indicates the two words that constitute a shorter format. The first: "Breathing in, I see myself as a mountain. Breathing out, I feel solid. Mountain/Solid."

You can silently recite the sutra while lying down, or sitting, or walking. If you want, you can just use the shortened form, saying "mountain" as you breathe in, and "solid" as you breathe out. There is a mountain in us; we are more solid and resilient than we think.

The second sutra focuses on calming turbulent waters: "Breathing in, I see myself as still water. Breathing out, I reflect things as they are. Water/Reflecting."

Again, the shorter form would be to say "water" while breathing in, and "reflecting" while breathing out. To find joy, we need to know how to stop our worries and anxieties. Reciting these sayings is a way of "stopping," or calming. If we want the ocean to be calm, Thich Nhat Hanh says, we do not get rid of its water. Likewise, we do not throw away the anger, fear, or agitation present in us. We soothe these strong emotions by consciously breathing in and out.

We are encouraged to practice "mountain/solid" or "water/reflecting" as often as we wish—five, ten, twenty, or more times a day—and not wait to do so until things become difficult. Reciting such sutras enables us to stop, calm ourselves, and come home to the present moment. Once we know how to soothe an emotion we are less likely to act hastily, without thinking.

To image this path to peace, Thich Nhat Hanh suggests that we picture a tree in a storm, noticing how at the top of the tree the wind is whipping the branches about violently. But at its trunk, and deeper still at its roots, the tree has the stability to resist the storm. As we sway about in the midst of emotional storms, we can survive if we are likewise firmly rooted. Rather than getting caught in the whirlwind of such strong emotions as despair, fear, anger, and jealousy, we return to the solid place where we quietly breathe in and out, developing strength and clarity. We sit like a mountain that no storm can blow down. Eventually joy comes again.

Being Awake

A few years ago my husband, Tom, and I were hiking the Naches Peak trail near Mt. Rainier. I remember feeling vague uneasiness when I realized we were the only hikers on this popular path. It was a Sunday afternoon in late August, and usually the trail would have had many hikers. *It's too quiet out here,* I remember thinking from time to time. *Something is not right.* But each time I scanned the hillside with a vague sense of discomfort, I overrode my misgivings and pressed on. When we returned to the trailhead, we encountered the first hikers we had seen. Did we meet up with the mother bear and her cubs? they wanted to know. Earlier hikers sighted her close to the path, and that was why they stayed at the trailhead. We risked an encounter with the bear because I failed to heed my immediate experience, taking in all that I was sensing about the situation and then acting on its message.

What we fear frequently happens when we are inattentive or reluctant to trust our intuition. We often put ourselves in harm's way while preoccupied with the past or future. Our monkey mind leaps from limb to limb, never staying long on any single branch, scattered and distracted when we need it most. In contrast, being fully connected with immediate experience produces gratitude and joy; it actually allays problems more effectively than worry and fear. It enables us to recognize goodness and beauty, along with evil and ugliness. We become fully engaged, attentive to the task at hand, more discerning in how to deal with it.

Such a spiritual path paradoxically eliminates the vague anxiety that plagues our days. What we are telling ourselves is this: we have within us the power to recognize real danger and take the actions necessary to prevent it. Paying attention also opens the way to the larger peace and unity we wish for our world.

Paying attention opens the way to the larger peace and unity we wish for our world.

We sometimes call such attentiveness *being fully awake*. Jesus made it the theme of many of his parables. Staying awake readies us to meet the Divine whenever and however it arrives, for God lies hidden within everyone and everything. The parables talk about daily activities similar to those described in mindfulness practice: a farmer doing seasonal work, sowing seeds and harvesting crops; people searching for items they've lost, getting married, or transacting business; brothers quarreling; and travelers getting into trouble on the road. We know these stories of God's extraordinary grace breaking into the ordinary as the parables of the Sower and the Seed, the Lost Coin, the Wedding Feast, the Talents, the Prodigal Son, and the Good Samaritan.

It is right where they are, in life's everyday details, that the characters in the parables discover the unexpected gifts of God. "Now the parable is this: The seed is the word of God. . . . But as for that in the good soil, these are the ones who, when they hear the word, hold it fast in an honest and good heart, and bear fruit with patient endurance" (Luke 8:11, 15).

The parables tell us to stay awake, for then we will recognize the in-breaking of grace in each moment. In fact, in the story of the wise and foolish virgins, we are told, "Keep awake therefore, for you know neither the day nor the hour" (Matt. 25:13). Many of us move through life as if sleepwalking, slightly unconscious much of the time. As soon as something is over—a cold, this job, college classes, a quarrel—we think the way will be clear for joy and contentment. But if we watch and pray, the parable says, keeping our lamps lit, they will illumine God's comings even now.

One of the many stories from the oral Zen tradition makes a similar point. A monk went to his master, complaining about the daily practices required of him to expand his capacity to be aware, to be mindful.

"What has all this to do with illumination?" the young disciple cried out. "Will it help me be illumined?"

"What you do will have as much effect on your illumination as it does on the sun rising," replied the master.

"Then why bother?" asked the young monk.

"Ah," came the reply, "so that you will be *awake* when the sun does rise."

Like poetry that reveals the depth in the ordinary, so also the parables of Jesus remind us that the help we are looking for when we are afraid, troubled, or weary is not far to seek. Here, the parables say, right in the here and now, you will discover the grace of courage and trust. You will learn not only how to work for peace, but how to *be* peace. In the midst of pain, fear, and suffering, you will come to recognize the wonder and abundance of creation. You will see life itself as a miracle. When, like Brother Lawrence in his kitchen, we open our hearts to the presence of God, all of life becomes a prayer. Then we can pull our scattered minds back from persistent worries about a troubled child, a

47

parent who drinks too much, or a bank account that will not balance, centering them on the experience at hand. Both mindfulness and the practice of the presence of God assure us that the future we desire arises from attentiveness to the present moment.

Chapter Four

Meditation as a Way to Peace

The only true joy on earth is to . . .
enter by love into union with the Life Who dwells
and sings within the essence of every creature
and in the core of our minds.

—THOMAS MERTON

A S A YOUNG MAN in his twenties, Thomas Merton looked on the spiritual life as an heroic endeavor that sets one apart from others. His decision, on the eve of World War II, to join the Trappist Abbey of Gethsemani in Kentucky reflected this desire to escape the world and live on a higher plane. But during his twenty-seven years at Gethsemani, Merton came to see the contemplative not as someone special and different, as he had believed in his youth. Rather, the contemplative is the person we might each become if we were released from the prison of the false self, the self distorted by fear, greed, and desperate desire. There exists, Merton believed, a source of identity that frees rather than restricts, enabling us to move through fear to a love of self and others. Contemplation takes us to this true and deepest identity that opens out into God and the universe.

Merton's personal journey to this center of freedom and joy was punctuated by brave struggles with anxiety, exhaustion, and disillusionment. From the solitude of his hermitage, he learned to identify with human frailty. He began to write not only on the spiritual life, but also on war and racism, peace and nonviolence. In these writings Merton speaks less as a stranger prophetically denouncing the world's sinfulness from a superior station than as one whose life is bound up with ours, a spiritual mentor cognizant of human weakness and of graced humanity as well: "There is no way of telling people that they are all walking around shining like the sun."

Merton grounded his spiritual quest in Christian tradition, but he also explored Eastern religions: Taoism, Buddhism, and Hinduism. These Eastern approaches opened for him unexpected perspectives on the spiritual life, revealing how much serious seekers from East and West hold in common. Shortly before his sudden death in 1968 at an international conference in Bangkok, Merton visited the Buddhas of Polonnaruwa in Ceylon. Approaching the figures barefoot in the wet grass and sand, he was deeply moved by the profound peace and silence he found in their smiling faces. He felt a great release of love and joy, a sense that he had found what he was seeking.

Merton's life is powerful witness to the Mystery sought by so many restless spiritual pilgrims. Longing for a sacred hearth lurks in the background of our days, like a melody we vaguely recognize yet never take time to sing.

But a number of meditation practices show us how to spend time regularly in this kind of awareness that we hope will gradually transform everyday consciousness. The term *meditation*, broadly used, describes a variety of spiritual approaches: Buddhist sitting meditation, Hindu mantra chanting, Christian centering prayer. Alike in that they invite us to a space of nondoing, of simply being in the moment, these disciplines over time calm the heart and mind, deepen compassion, and open us to the Spirit that dwells in us and all creation. Meditation brings us home to the hearth.

Meditation practices also still the restless heart, providing a more lasting path to peace than the worry and anxiety that seem to protect us from danger. Some part of us believes that worrying long and hard enough will prevent bad things from happening, the way a sentinel's constant surveillance stops an enemy from reaching a fortress. Prepare for the worst by continually focusing on it, we tell ourselves. Meditation, on the other hand, takes a paradoxical approach: prepare for the worst by *not* thinking about it all the time. Experience each moment, knowing that it is the only thing you truly have, and that when trouble comes, you will be given in *that* moment the wisdom and strength you need to deal with it.

Meditation practices still the restless heart, providing a more lasting path to peace than the anxiety that seems to protect us from danger.

51

If meditation is something you would like as a part of your spirituality, consider beginning or deepening one of the practices described here.

Mindfulness Meditation

The ancient Buddhist practice of mindfulness meditation fosters awareness of the present moment in a systematic way. It cultivates the ability to be truly awake rather than simply moving unconsciously through life. In meditation we step back from the stream of thoughts and emotions rushing through us. We listen and learn from them, and then know better how to direct these feelings.

Though rooted in Buddhism, mindfulness practice appeals to people from a variety of religious traditions. It does not conflict with any beliefs, and a person need not be a Buddhist to practice it. The word *Buddha* actually means one who has awakened to his or her true nature. Many spiritual seekers find that mindfulness practice leads to conscious, intentional living, as well as to a compassionate outreach to others. It opens the heart, preparing one for the silent presence of God. A Christian friend of mine who has done this kind of meditation for years is often described by others in this way: "She is so completely present to everyone and everything."

To try this practice, choose a place where you will not be interrupted, and a posture that allows you to be alert but comfortable. You can sit, stand, walk, or lie down (so long as you are not likely to fall asleep). Some teachers suggest adopting a position by thinking of yourself as a mountain, grounded and erect, but not stiff or tense. Close your

eyes and begin to notice your breath. In meditating, we
need a focal point for attention, an anchor to return to
whenever the mind begins to wander. The breath works
very well for this.

Do not try to change your breath; just follow it,
noticing the feeling of it. Become aware of it moving in and
moving out. If you find yourself distracted by other things,
just return gently, with the lightest sort of touch, to awareness of your breathing. The heart of this path of meditating
is use of the breath, or some other focal point such as bodily
sensations, to bring you back to the present moment.
Attending to the breath fosters a sense that this is it, this is
life. If other thoughts or feelings arise, accept whatever
comes without judgment, as you might regard a ship passing on the horizon.

The hardest part of any meditation practice is staying with it. Your mind will jump around and chatter nervously, or spin like a pinwheel. You will feel tempted to give
up. As in life, so in meditation, many concerns clutter your
mind and call out for attention. Suppose tears or feelings of
grief arise, or you find yourself remembering a conversation
with a friend and getting angry. Simply let yourself notice
these feelings and then quietly return your attention to your
breath. If you are doing walking meditation (which is just as
good as sitting meditation), see if you can attend to each
step and each breath.

Think of mindfulness practice as nurturing and
gentle, not harsh or judgmental. You don't have to strain to
feel a certain way (for example, to be relaxed, or have an
empty mind). Calmness may come, but not by seeking it

directly. Rather, it flows from the commitment to being in the stillness. Continue your time of practice for as long as you wish; it may help to start with a shorter period, moving from five to ten, to fifteen or twenty minutes.

In addition to use of the breath, mindfulness meditation can have a specific area of experience as its focus. In sessions of this kind, rather than turning your attention away from feelings, you consciously meditate on them. Such meditation is a way of noticing how an emotion affects you, listening deeply for answers from body, mind, and heart. For example, try reflecting on something that scares you.

Sit quietly, noticing the movement of your breath in your body. Let yourself come into a receptive place, and then become aware of some fear that you face in your life. It may be an approaching task, an upcoming transition, a health problem, or concern for your children. Notice how it is manifesting itself in your body and mind. Watch how it rises and falls, and what other feelings (such as shame or anger) come with it. Feel it as fully as possible, and then ask yourself:

What am I most deeply afraid of in this matter?
How have I treated the fear so far?
What has resulted from my response?
What can I change, and what am I called to accept?
How can this fear teach me?

Let the answers come from within, and give them whatever time they need to appear. What you are seeking is direct engagement with your present bodily experience. You are not so much concerned with avoiding or analyzing uncertainty and fear as with how to relate to them.

Pema Chödrön believes that life's circumstances can either harden and frighten us, or make us kind and wise. The trick, she says, is to let emotional distress soften us rather than turn into resistance. We shield ourselves from the pain that scares us by erecting barriers against what hurts. These defenses appear as jealousy, prejudice, violence, or arrogance. Beyond our fear, Chödrön sees a state of openheartedness: "Compassion practice is daring. It involves learning to relax and allow ourselves to move gently toward what scares us." The practice of meditation offers one way to mend the broken heart that so often expresses itself in anxiety and panic, and to uncover instead our innate capacity for courage and love.

Because greater calm and reduced anxiety often occur as a side effect of mindfulness practice, its effects have drawn increased interest from researchers in recent years. In fact, this research documents the power of meditation to transform us over time at a deep physical and psychic level. Meditation increases our capacity to tolerate the feeling of fear in our body; it teaches us how to experience it and let it go. Meditation even brings more immediate physiological changes, such as lowered blood pressure and a stronger immune system. For these reasons, mindfulness practice now finds a place in many health care programs, pain management centers, and therapy training seminars.

Centering Prayer

Buddhists do not refer to mindfulness meditation as *prayer*, since belief in God is not an intrinsic part of it. But faith in the Divine does define the contemplative path called *centering prayer.* There are similarities in the methods recommended for both practices. In centering prayer, as in mindfulness meditation, our attention turns for a time from the flow of ordinary consciousness. By doing so, it opens more fully to the presence of God. This gradually helps us remain more attuned at other times to the Divine Spirit in whom we "live and move and have our being" (Acts 17:28). We then carry contemplation into all of our actions.

The practice of centering prayer takes a variety of forms and can differ in its details. Methods of prayer are secondary in any case; they are simply ways of making ourselves available to God. So we try not to let ourselves get caught up in worrying about the best way to pray. We allow ourselves to walk the path that works best for us, trusting that God remains larger than any technique. A man in his seventies, a resident in a nursing center where I worked, had this kind of freedom in approaches to prayer. He told me how he dealt with the fear of dying that would come over him at times; he would "repeat the Lord's Prayer over and over like a chant. Sometimes it even carries itself. It's the rhythm— like water and waves moving in and out. I can't think of another thing while I'm doing that."

Methods of prayer are ways of making ourselves available to God.

A form of centering prayer that many find helpful is based on the fourteenth-century classic *The Cloud of Unknowing.* It relies on a short word to hold us in God's presence. Choose a word that expresses something of how you image the divine or how you see your relationship to God. A word such as Mercy, Love, Peace, Beloved, Water, or Sophia might appeal to you.

Once you have chosen this anchoring word, find a quiet place where you will not be disturbed. A silent location best supports meditation, but I have also meditated on buses, planes, trains, and benches in noisy parks. Take a posture similar to that described for mindfulness meditation, one in which you are open and alert but relaxed in body and mind. You might spend a moment or two consciously letting go of other concerns and allowing your body to relax.

Then close your eyes. Recall that you are in God's presence. When I do centering prayer, I begin by saying, "Spirit of the Living God, I am here to spend some time with you." Or you might call to mind the biblical text, "Be still, and know that I am God" (Ps. 46:10). Then simply rest in God. Whenever you find yourself thinking, imaging, feeling, or focusing on anything else, gently repeat your word (Beloved, Mercy, Water) to bring you back to this presence. This may be necessary quite often, even many times in a moment, especially when life is busy or difficult. The suggested time for centering prayer is twenty minutes, twice a day when possible. This is about the time it takes to move to a deeper level of prayer. But people center for longer or shorter periods, and many can manage only one session a day. When you are ready to end your meditation, open your eyes and come back to your surroundings. If you like, end with a familiar prayer.

This method of centering prayer can be summarized in this way:

1. Choose beforehand a short word to anchor you in God's presence.
2. Find a quiet place and a comfortable posture.
3. Close your eyes and open yourself to the Divine presence.
4. Whenever you find your thoughts wandering, gently return to your word.
5. Close your meditation time with a favorite prayer.

Centering prayer strengthens us to face the challenges of each day. Basil Pennington, a Trappist monk who helped revive this ancient prayer practice, describes how the compassion that grew in him through his contemplation differed from his previous efforts to enter into others' suffering. Pennington worked in a Brooklyn parish that averaged a murder a night. At the end of each day, he anguished over how to respond to the needs surrounding him on every side: "I felt I was going to be torn to pieces, to be completely consumed in trying to respond to each one."

Through centering prayer, Pennington found that an experience of the Spirit of God accompanied him in his sense of oneness with others' pain. No longer dependent solely on his own resources, but now relying more on the power of the love of God, he was able to respond peacefully to each person. Once he began to realize that the Spirit of Love is in us as our own Spirit, Pennington could ride the buses in Boston and New York and take in the anguish on people's faces without being totally drained.

But Can *I* Meditate?

By this time you may be saying, "I don't have a minute to spare in my schedule." Or "I couldn't possibly stay with a daily practice." Or "There is no way I can just sit and do nothing." During years of being a spiritual companion to people from diverse backgrounds, I have discovered how many people long for the stillness of contemplative prayer but consider it beyond their reach. For one thing, the modern focus on productivity interferes with commitment to daily meditation. We believe the time could instead be used to get things done. A woman who came to me for spiritual direction found that she could meditate only if she did it the very first thing in the morning, with as much regularity as brushing her teeth. If she let herself think about whether or not to do it, urgency about all the other projects she had to complete rushed in to overwhelm her resolve.

Even so, lack of time can sometimes be a real obstacle. Most days, especially for parents raising small children, are filled to the brim. But something is better than nothing. One moment of centering may be all that we can manage, but that moment may easily expand to others. Another paradoxical truth concerns time. Setting aside several moments each day for simply being rather than doing changes the flow of everything else. Daily life takes on another quality. As we shift our priorities to make room for meditation, we may find both time and energy to do other things more effectively. It is also important to remember that a set schedule for formal meditation is a means and not an end. It is often more difficult to change diapers, cook supper, or deal with anger at a colleague than it is to chant a mantra or return to an anchoring word. Each task can itself become an opportunity for awareness or prayer. Many paths point the way to peace and holiness.

Most of us carry a slightly romantic notion of prayerful people. We think we ought to feel a certain way during prayer. We imagine that others—those who meditate much better than we do—experience comfort, joy, inner quiet, or a clear sense of God's presence each time they pray. We find ourselves restless, impatient, scattered, or flat and we attribute it to our own deficits. If we are perfectionists (as many anxious people are), we become concerned that we are just not doing it right. So we either try harder or give up completely.

It is not how we are feeling when we are meditating, but how we love when we are living that constitutes the yardstick for prayer.

But a central piece of wisdom recurs throughout writings on prayer: do not seek the results of prayer within the practice itself. It is not how we are feeling when we are meditating, but how we love when we are living that constitutes the yardstick for prayer. The fruits of contemplation arrive as gifts of the Spirit, and they show up more reliably from day to day than in set prayer periods.

Although contemplation will transform us over time, on a daily basis distraction, boredom, or an unremarkable dryness often marks our prayer. Very holy people strug-

gle with emptiness and discouragement in their prayer.
What sets them apart is the fact that they keep returning
to it. The touchstone of centering prayer is still a life
that reflects what it means to be in relationship with God.
This follows the pattern of Jesus and God's prophets and
saints. Again and again, we bring ourselves into the presence of God, and we let God gradually change us. This
usually happens without our knowing it, which is probably
a good thing.

Meditating in the company of others helps, and
centering prayer is frequently practiced in community. This
enables an individual to share in the commitment of the
group and supports the desire to be faithful to prayer.
Finally, because the spiritual journey can take confusing
twists and turns, many serious spiritual seekers choose
someone as a companion on the quest. This person, vari-
ously known as a guru, Zen master, spiritual director, or
spiritual friend, listens with us to the Spirit's movement in
our lives. In many ways, meeting with a spiritual guide
resembles shared meditation or prayer. In the company of a
spiritual friend, we find our way through questions that
arise, and we learn to weave spiritual practices into the reality of our actual life. Sometimes meditation uncovers layers
of pain that call for professional help. In this case, a therapist may be the appropriate companion, since spiritual
guides may not be trained to deal with these more serious or
complicated issues inviting us to deeper healing.

As a mentor whose writings continue to have a
major influence on many spiritual journeys, Merton brings
us back to a key truth about meditation and peace. Though

meditation may happen in solitude, when practiced truly it does not isolate. When it takes me to my center and heart, to God and my self, I also discover there the true peace of communion with all reality. In a talk Merton gave in Calcutta a few weeks before he died, he spoke of this union. It is not, he said, as though we discover a new unity. Rather, we realize an older one. We are already one, though we imagine we are not:

Meditation takes me to my center and heart, to God and my self, where I also discover the true peace of communion with all reality.

"And what we have to recover is our original unity. What we have to be is what we are." The intuition of the oneness of all reality takes us beyond surface divisions. We find in God not only our own heart and inner truth but all our brothers and sisters in the universe as well.

Chapter Five

Praying When We're Scared

Ultimately, we have just one moral duty: to reclaim large areas of peace in ourselves, more and more peace, and to reflect it towards others. And the more peace there is in us, the more peace there will also be in our troubled world.

—ETTY HILLESUM

FANNIE LOU HAMER, one of twenty children of a poor sharecropper in the Mississippi Delta, taught others to turn fear into prayer. Hamer worked in the fields picking cotton until 1962, when she attended a rally where a preacher issued a summons for blacks to register to vote. Answering this call plunged her into the freedom movement full-time at the age of forty-five, eventually transforming her into a leader whose courage inspired many followers. Deeply rooted in biblical faith, Hamer and her companions managed to stand up to clubs, fire hoses, dogs, bombs, and savage beatings. In spite of these beatings, which left her with permanent impairment of vision in her left eye, Hamer refused to give in to hatred:

"I feel sorry for anybody that could let hate wrap them up. Ain't no such thing as I can hate anybody and hope to see God's face." Hamer found strength in the God of the oppressed. Pushing past fear, she put new words to old songs of faith, like "This Little Light of Mine": "All over the Delta, I'm gonna let it shine. . . . Let it shine, let it shine, let it shine!"

Like Hamer, saints and prophets from diverse spiritual traditions have gone down on their knees to plead for assistance, rising to meet tremendous challenges. So have ordinary people who deal daily with less heroic measures of courage. When we appeal to the Divine at such times, it is acknowledgment of the encompassing Mercy that grounds our existence. Why should that Love not provide a place of refuge when courage falters and resources give way? Turning to God when we're scared comes as naturally to human beings as breathing. Some deride this kind of prayer as a remnant of childish belief, a knee-jerk reaction to vulnerability. But petition becomes too narrow a path of prayer only if we pray that way exclusively. Crying "Help me!" when we are afraid constitutes a spiritual problem only if we also fail to say "Thank you!" Both have a place in an integral spiritual life.

Turning to God when we're scared comes as naturally to human beings as breathing.

But how shall we pray when we are anxious or afraid? As fear grips the mind and body, certain forms of prayer become impossible. Others rise right from where we are, comforting and grounding us, giving us strength.

The Rhythm of Repetition

Sometimes we are plagued not so much by specific fears as by an ill-defined unease, a restless anxiety. Moment by moment, we search the horizon for potential trouble, as a computer scans its files for viruses. This anxiety flits from one subject to another: Will my son make it to school safely? Is the spring flooding going to reach our house? What if my doctor finds something terminal during my next physical? Like carpenter ants gnawing at the foundation of a house, these relentless worries eat away at inner peace.

Further, fear talks to us, and we talk back. "I think I'll hike the Pacific Trail," you say. "What?" fear replies; "You'll have to camp in the cold rain, and the woods will be full of bears and mosquitoes." Or "I'm going to accept Sally's party invitation," you decide. Fear takes up the challenge: "You'll have to talk to a bunch of strangers, and you'll have nothing to say. They'll think you're a loser. Better stay home."

Modern psychotherapy addresses this kind of anxiety. It tells us that we can change our emotions by changing our inner dialogue. Convinced that our thoughts shape emotions such as fear, cognitive behavioral therapy tries to reduce fear by putting a new interpretation on events that scare us. In the same way that a picture frame determines what we see, so also how we view events influences our feelings about them.

Consider a person preparing to give a presentation. If his inner self-talk revolves around what he does not know and how critical the listeners will be, his anxiety will rise. On the other hand, positive thoughts about his preparedness and gifts will help calm him for the task. We tend to become anxious before a performance if we envision others being judgmental and critical. Thinking of a potential audience as composed of fallible people with marriage problems and household debt modifies the frightening image. Proponents of this kind of therapy believe it is not the events themselves but rather what we tell ourselves about them that makes the difference between trust and turmoil.

Ancient spiritual wisdom actually anticipated these modern therapeutic approaches to reducing anxiety. It offers kinds of prayer that situate danger in the context of divine care and assistance, offering a sacred refuge when we are scared. Repetition of short words or phrases allows prayer to move quietly beneath conscious thought to the layers of anger, sadness, and fear within us, like fog rolling gently in from the sea.

Consider how the poetry of the Psalms returns to a theme, washing over our fears again and again:

> *How precious is your steadfast love, O God!*
> *All people may take refuge in the shadow of*
>   *your wings.*
>
> —Psalm 36:7

In God, whose word I praise,
in God I trust; I am not afraid;
what can flesh do to me?

   —Psalm 56:4

Hear my cry, O God;
listen to my prayer.
From the end of the earth I call to you,
when my heart is faint.

   —Psalm 61:1–2

Repeating such verses, or similar short prayers we compose for ourselves, gradually replaces the anxious self-talk that becomes habitual. These prayers transfigure the heart, easing the worries that preoccupy it. In the same way, chanting, litany, and the use of prayer beads—practices found in many spiritual traditions—ground us in times of trouble.

Chanting, litany, and the use of prayer beads—practices found in many spiritual traditions—ground us in times of trouble.

From the spirituality of the fifth and sixth centuries comes a practice of repeating a phrase so often that it eventually becomes a part of oneself. It is known as prayer of the heart, or *Hesychasm*. The term is derived from the Greek word for quiet or stillness. Four elements distinguish this spirituality: devotion to the name of Jesus, sorrow for sin, the discipline of frequent repetition, and imageless prayer that leads to inner silence. Based on a strong affirmation of the divine presence in all of creation, Hesychasm teaches that human beings must above all come to know God if they are to avoid distorting their own being and the world in which they live.

This tradition's best-known prayer is the Jesus Prayer: "Lord Jesus Christ, Son of God, have mercy on me." We focus inwardly on the place of the heart, while calming the breath to match the quiet rhythm of prayer. With the heart and mind thus joined, the Jesus Prayer is repeated as a way of keeping guard over the heart. Its refrain of sorrow for sin and plea for forgiveness opens us to the imageless prayer of inner silence. Repetition blocks out all impulses aside from this silence. God is then found in an emptiness that lies beyond image, thought, and symbol. As with all forms of centering prayer, the refrain may shorten or disappear altogether as it is repeated. We become aware of distractions, but we simply return gently to the prayer.

A client describes how this path of prayer enabled her to hear criticism of her work without being paralyzed by fear: "All my life I've been filled with anxiety. I tried to deal with it by avoiding more and more situations, but that didn't work. Then I discovered the prayer of the heart. It gave me a container for my fear, and now I can face into that dread without feeling like it will take over." An emphasis on the heart as a dwelling place for the divine occurs as well in the Islamic belief that even though heaven and earth cannot contain God, the human heart can.

Release Through Movement

A young woman who began the practice of tai chi explained her choice of an active path to greater calm: "I've been anxious all my life, and when I try to meditate there's just me and my brain, and together we manage to make things worse. So you won't see me doing any meditating." Anxiety renders us restless; we cannot sit still long enough to pray as we have been taught we should. Fear takes over the body and mind, leaving us shut down and speechless. At such times we wring our hands. We grimace. We pace. We sigh. We find it hard to concentrate or focus. As we saw earlier in reflecting on the nature of fear, it involves the rush of energizing chemicals to muscles and mind, preparing us to confront danger. Because of this, prayer that requires us to pretend we are peaceful may simply give anxiety greater scope. Here is where the long history of movement in prayer helps.

Walking meditation has an honored place in many traditions. Most recently, the labyrinth walking meditation has been rediscovered, yielding a way of finding stillness in stressful times. An inheritance from the Middle Ages, the labyrinth has attracted spiritual pilgrims from many religious backgrounds. Labyrinths are usually shaped like a circle, with a path from the outer edge to the center and back out again. A labyrinth offers only one path, large enough to walk on, and it serves as a metaphor for our life passage. The original design for the best-known example of the classical eleven-circuit labyrinth comes from the floor of the twelfth-century Chartres Cathedral in France.

Walking a labyrinth often brings a sense of peace and possibility. A way of connecting with the Divine, it awakens and deepens. In *Walking a Sacred Path*, Lauren Artress tells how a woman who felt deep alienation because of incest in her family wanted to walk the labyrinth. Afraid that walking it alone would intensify her feelings of isolation, she invited a friend to join her. The woman wept as they moved toward the center. Many of the fears of her past were present to her, but the walking helped her continue her journey of healing.

Body prayer also works well in times of fear. When I taught courses on prayer and spirituality, I invited a liturgical dancer to do several sessions that she called "The Body in Prayer." I remember how freeing it was to pray with the body. You can begin by scanning your body, listening for tightness, knots, and discomfort. Then let that part of your body speak your prayer. Simply move into a posture that expresses it. For example, if your chest is tight with fear, lift your heart slightly, opening it as much as you can to Light and Life. If your arms and shoulders are tense, slowly extend them several times to embrace the sun, moon, and stars, welcoming the warm and sustaining embrace of the creation and its Creator.

Put your prayer in the first person, and let that part of your body speak: "I am so afraid for myself and the world. When I think of all that is wrong, I despair of fixing it. So I cannot let myself really relax and feel joy. There is too much weighing on my heart, and I am anxious all the time." As you say this prayer, let your body posture interpret the words. Lie prostrate and reach out your arms in fear and pleading. Slump or collapse your body forward, and lie in a pose of despair. Clutch your hands to your chest as you describe the weight on your heart. You might then close with a prayer of trust during which you release and relax each part of your body, perhaps taking a few steps in a prayerful and joyful dance of your own making.

Another way of bringing your body into prayer is to move freely to the words of a favorite psalm or hymn. Or wordlessly take the posture that best expresses where you are right now: prostrate in supplication, tightly bound in fear, arms extended in pleading or praise. You may want to include traditional bodily gestures such as kneeling or bowing.

Performing Rituals

A Hasidic tale relates that when an only child of parents in a village was in danger of death, the Baal Shem Tov, the founder of Hasidic Judaism, had someone make him a candle, and then he journeyed into the forest to light it and say various prayers for the boy. The child was saved. Some years later, a similarly grave matter arose, and his disciple did as the Baal Shem Tov had done; he remarked, "I don't know all the prayers that he said before me, but I'll simply act, relying on the intentions our founder had in his meditations." This was acceptable to God and had the desired effect. Still later, his successor faced a similar crisis, and he said, "I don't have the ability to do what is necessary, but I'll just tell the story, and God will help." With God's help, it was enough.

When tragedy threatens, we often turn hopefully to the familiar rituals of a community of faith. We draw power from these symbols and sacraments, and from the faith of those gathered in prayer. Sometimes, however, we are on our own, without traditional rituals to turn to; then our symbolic action may be spontaneous and spare. We can only light a candle, tell a story, gesture, sob, or scream. It suffices.

In the absence of established ritual, or as a supplement to it, we can create our own symbolic actions. When my brother-in-law had surgery for prostate cancer, he said he went into the procedure without fear after the ritual we did with him. I remember the palpable level of anxiety permeating the waiting area when we arrived. People huddled in small groups with those preparing for surgery, their unease accentuated by lack of sleep, the bright lighting of the area, and the pre-op preparations. In the midst of this, we found time and a private space to do a simple ritual with my brother-in-law. We all laid hands on him, praying for healing. We prayed for his surgeons and all who would assist him. We asked him to take in the love of all those who were remembering him at this time. Then we recited a litany we had composed to ask for strength, safety, and healing.

We also need ritual that speaks to larger communal fears, especially when dread of impending disaster defines the global mood (as it does now). In her book *Healing Through the Dark Emotions*, Miriam Greenspan offers such an exercise, which she calls "Dark Emotions in the World." The ritual can be done alone or in groups. It opens with placing objects in the four corners of the room to symbolize the grief, fear, despair, and anger in the world. Greenspan suggests an autumn leaf to symbolize grief, a rock for fear, a stick for anger, and a crystal to stand for the world's despair.

Once these symbols are in place, each corner becomes the focus of silent contemplation. Alone, or with others, quietly contemplate first the grief in the world at this time. Bring to mind the sorrow you have seen or heard in the news. Lift up also the grief you have in your own heart for the violence and conflict in the universe. Then open your eyes and write or create something out of your sorrow. Pray for guidance to know what you can do to ease the world's grief.

Follow this same movement of prayer for the other three corners. If you are in a group, speak and hear the fruits of one another's contemplation of these emotions. Greenspan suggests that a closing personal or group prayer might go something like this: "May the world be liberated from its suffering. May I use my own pain to grow in compassion. May we learn, and help one another learn, how to heal and redeem the world's suffering. Amen."

Praying in the Dark

Early one evening in the summer of 2003, I was in the kitchen getting supper ready, when suddenly dozens of floaters and squiggles of various sizes and shapes filled my left eye. Along with these floaters came the sensation of light flashes and lightning streaks, like shooting stars or a summer light show. Afraid I was losing my mind, I sank into a chair and sat until the episode subsided. When I saw my eye doctor, I learned that I had a vitreous detachment, a condition caused by shrinkage of the fluid in my eye. Because the process was not going smoothly, I was at risk of losing sight in that eye.

During the months I waited for the condition to stabilize, I experienced a new kind of fear of the dark. Whenever I entered a dim room, the flashes and streaks I saw were visible reminders that I might lose my sight. Consequently I began to dread entering any dimly lit space. Every night I had to pray my way into the bedroom, bathroom, or kitchen, each time resisting the urge to simply leave the lights on rather than face the fear of the dark.

Fears magnify in the dark, so night (along with other bleak times) calls for prayer that takes this into account. A mother whom I saw in spiritual direction recounts how she prayed all night for her daughter, who was struggling with depression and contemplating suicide. "Finally," she said, "comfort came like a breaking fever. I had prayed to Our Lady of Guadalupe and I heard her reply in the words she said to Juan Diego: 'Am I not present there for you as your mother?' I was able to fall asleep, putting my trust in that message."

Fear that accompanies darkness responds best to the familiar. Lines of prayer or poetry already memorized, the hymn many times sung, the lighted candle simply lit—these all bring benediction. If nothing comes to you, you might try this night chant, addressing God by a name that fits for you, such as Mercy, Beloved, or Spirit.

> *Merciful God, you tell us not to be afraid,*
> *for even in the darkest valley,*
> *you will be with us.*
>
> *Abide with me.*
> *Dusk falls,*

and the shadows deepen,
the light departs.
Abide with me.

Give me hope.
Despair descends,
my options are few,
no path seems clear.
Give me hope.

Lift me up.
Courage falters,
my faith weakens,
my reserves fail.
Lift me up.

Light my way.
Vision dims,
my fear builds,
signposts vanish.
Light my way.

Abide with me.
Give me hope.
Lift me up.
Light my way.

The last stanza can then be repeated with whatever words you want to add.

Writing our prayers unravels apprehension and brings perspective. A common suggestion for anxiety that keeps us awake at night is to describe it briefly in a prayer journal, which we then place next to our bed, and turn it all over to God until morning.

Finding Solace When We're Alone

Fear is often at its worst when we're alone. A friend who sometimes has what she calls "night terrors"—a magnified sense of the threatening aspects of her life during the night—finds that these fears strike most forcefully whenever her husband is away on a business trip.

Sometimes, however, we cannot avoid being alone; others cannot always be physically at our side. Prayer that evokes the presence of trusted loved ones can support us even then. As we make our way through frightening experiences—an impending diagnosis, a troubling family visit, or a challenging professional meeting—a meditation that draws on the support of others can be helpful. Close your eyes and picture yourself in a calming place—near the ocean, in a meadow, in a favorite room. Then invite, one by one, wise people whose love you trust to form a circle around you. These wisdom figures can be living or dead, religious or not. People sometimes choose Jesus or Mary of Nazareth, a favorite saint such as Francis of Assisi, grandparents and parents, friends and mentors. Once you have filled out the circle, simply be in the encompassing presence and take in anything that

Prayer that evokes the presence of trusted loved ones can support us when we are alone.

comes to you. Sometimes it is merely a sense of love and comfort. At other times there is shared wisdom ("Be strong." "I have been there and I understand." "Trust your gifts." "You are Beloved of God."). Remember that you can return to the meditation at a later time, again drawing strength from it.

Imploring Help for Ourselves and Others

Jesus' words in the Garden of Gethsemane are a model for Christian prayer of petition. Faced with his impending suffering and death, Jesus is so scared, the gospel writers tell us, that his sweat turns into drops of blood. From that place of loneliness, he cries out to be delivered from the pain. But if this is not possible, then he will surrender to God's larger purpose.

Jesus shows great freedom in asking for exactly what he wants and needs: release from his present agony and the torture that awaits him. Then he recognizes that God's wisdom may be deeper than his own prayer. This is how we are to pray: laying out our heart's longings as honestly as we can, and then acknowledging that the answers may come in ways we cannot anticipate and that we may barely recognize when they arrive. After several weeks of obvious distress over the state of the world, my husband, Tom, suddenly found a much more peaceful place to be. I asked what had happened. "I have to let God be God," he said. In each of the major spiritual traditions, there is a point in prayer where peace comes from surrendering to a larger Reality. We relinquish control. We give up trying to understand or change things very much.

It is hard to accept how little we can do to protect those we love from the dangers lurking everywhere. Children have car accidents. Spouses get cancer. Friends die. Allowing those close to us to live freely in the world requires that we release them into the care of a compassionate Presence, a God who wants their well-being as much as we do. An ancient blessing from the biblical book of Numbers (6: 24–26) turns our fears to prayer:

> *The Lord bless you and keep you;*
> *the Lord make his face to shine*
> *upon you, and be gracious to you;*
> *the Lord lift up his countenance*
> *upon you, and give you peace.*

Praying with the Imagination

Like anger, fear draws its fuel from the imagination. We play movies in our mind, concocting scenes of disaster. The media augments this process by supplying images of tragedy from around the globe, vivid pictures that lodge in our mind, stirring our emotions. A mother became aware of this when her two daughters were describing their cheerleading class. They remarked that in the class they had to raise their arms and hold them above their head for a long time. It got painful. Then they asked whether this was a method of torture in the world. They wondered whether, should they ever be tortured in that way, they would be able to stand it. The mother commented to me: "Did I think like that as a kid? No way."

Praying with the imagination counters such frightening images of the future; it supports creativity, courage, and action for change. Here are two possible ways of doing it.

Let yourself enter a biblical passage that increases trust, and stay in it to receive its graces. The passage where Jesus falls asleep in the boat with his disciples is a favorite of mine. It captures the sense that God seems absent just when we need help most. First, read through the account in Mark 4:35–40. Then get in the boat with Jesus and the other disciples. Watch evening deepen as you leave the crowds on the shore behind and head out onto the water. Then feel the wind as it whips up the waters, tossing the boat about mercilessly. Feel the waters swamp the boat and the terror that arises as you think it is about to sink. What do you experience as you notice that Jesus is in the stern, asleep on a cushion? Then he awakens, rebukes the wind and sea, and calls out, "Peace. Be still!" Can you take in these words? Stay with that complete and sudden calm, and let your imagination soak up the possibility of it. Let it wash over your anxiety and fear. Then express any prayers that come to you.

Praying with the imagination counters frightening images of the future; it supports creativity, courage, and action for change.

Another way to change the movies within your mind is to take a moment to create the kind of world you want for yourself and others. Imagine all people living at peace with one another. See the forests filled with trees again, and the rivers running clean and clear. Replace the homeless on the streets with cities that house and feed all people. Let yourself roam unafraid and happy in their midst. Hope and despair are, after all, both choices that tend to bring about what they envision. Praying this way allows a new world to become a reality in our hearts, and eventually in our actions.

Chapter Six

Finding Hope in Difficult Times

Hope's home is at the innermost point in us,
and in all things.

—CYNTHIA BOURGEAULT

WHILE ON A LATE WINTER'S WALK one afternoon, my husband and I paused to study several poplar trees filled with red-winged blackbirds. As we watched, these recently hatched aviators swooped to the branches in large flocks, energizing the area with their chatter. "Watch their flight experiments," Tom said. "They're just discovering they can fly." Perched on thin, bare branches, the blackbirds seemed impervious to the fact that spring had not yet fully arrived, and by sunset this sunny February day would give way to a frigid night. Neither past struggle nor future hazard dampened their excitement.

Along with all of nature, we live by hope. It is therefore not surprising that researchers interested in helping people cope with anxiety have recently focused on the link between fear and hope. As might be expected, studies show that individuals who struggle with anxiety find it hard to hope. But as hope increases, fear recedes. For one thing, hope eases hypervigilance, since it views the future as more promising than threatening. Hopeful people do not become reckless, but they are less prone to false alarms. Hope also fosters more favorable appraisal of our ability to overcome obstacles. Hope retains a sense of the possible; it sees a way out of difficulty.

Any situation offers the option of hope or despair, because no one actually knows the future. But the choices we make contribute to the very scenarios we envision. We frequently refer to this as *self-fulfilling prophecy*. If fear is constantly aroused without any resolution, a state of apathy results. In this uncaring condition a person becomes indifferent, ceases to try, and feels no desire to shape the future. Goals seem impossible to achieve, so why bother? Future outcomes then reflect this stance. Hope, on the other hand, helps to create the future we desire. Like a trusted Sherpa guide clearing a path through tough terrain, hope enables us to surmount the obstacles blocking us.

> As *hope increases, fear recedes.*

Who would not want to experience such hope, especially in the grip of chronic anxiety? But where can it be found?

Spiritual traditions indicate that hope already lives in and around us. Just as moonlight casts its reassuring light on forests and meadows, so hope hovers at the edge of our darkest landscape. Anxiety gives way to grace as we take in these hopeful moments wherever they greet us. A woman devastated by news that her husband is divorcing her finds that her friends believe she can make it on her own. A doctor tells parents struggling with a child's depression that treatments exist that will help. We plant pencil-thin mock oranges, and three springs later we find large bushes with fragrant white blossoms. A war-torn region of the world moves a step closer to peace. Loggers and environmentalists work together to save a section of old-growth forest. Just so does the Spirit of God offer hope to a fractured world. As Paul tells the early Christians in his letter to the Romans, we who have the first fruits of the Spirit eagerly await with all creation the fullness of redemption. In the meantime, we are saved by hope (8:18–25).

When we are broken and bereft, prophets and poets offer us images of the future that God is preparing for us. In the grip of fear, we learn to remember the past hopefully rather than restrictively. Longing for inner healing, we find that stories of faith engender courage and resilience.

Imagining a Positive Future

In the summer of 1971, during the protracted and divisive Vietnam War, John Lennon wrote his song "Imagine." In it he asks us to envision a universal community of people at peace. Lennon knew he might be called a dreamer for even entertaining the possibility of such a world, but he believed others shared his hopeful vision. In fact, poets and prophets before and after Lennon have urged us to keep our imagination just so alive. Should we become disillusioned and afraid, we find strength by picturing how we want things to be. Future survival depends on the capacity to rehearse alternate possibilities for existence, and it is the imagination that opens up such prospects. Nothing becomes possible until we have first imagined it; images contain the future that is waiting to come into being.

The Hebrew Scriptures make this point incisively. In 587 B.C.E., Babylon conquered Jerusalem, destroying the holy city and the symbols that defined Judah as a people. The temple lay in ruins, the Davidic dynasty was over, and the leading citizens were deported to Babylon. Thus began the period known as the Babylonian Exile. Hope drained from people's hearts. The world they knew had ended. The task of keeping Israel from despair fell to such prophets as Jeremiah, Ezekiel, and Isaiah. In a language consisting largely of poetry, they appealed to the imagination of a community.

Before we can hope, we often need to grieve the losses, pain, and confusion that block hope's way. We may also need to repent. The prophets courageously called their people to conversion, refusing to let them dwell in denial. The community had lost a sense of the holiness of God, and they no longer showed compassion for others. Injustice, calculation, and dishonesty marked their interactions. They needed to grieve for what they had been and what they had lost before they could open to the new world God would give them.

The prophets' vision of a hopeful future transformed the familiar symbols of Israel's past. Out of a broken tradition came fresh metaphors: a restored Garden of Eden, a reclaimed temple, a new David, a fresh way through the desert. But most of all, God promised to transform their hearts in a way they seemed incapable of doing themselves: "A new heart I will give you, and a new spirit I will put within you; and I will remove from your body the heart of stone and give you a heart of flesh" (Ezek. 36:26). In exile, with all hope seemingly gone, the poetry of the prophets reconfigured the communal images that had sustained Israel in the past.

Throughout the centuries, this poetry has also inspired hope in those who relive the stories of exodus and exile. In desolation and darkness, we turn to the promise of deserts blossoming. In rejection and failure, we trust that we will find release from exile and recover a lost homeland. Entire peoples dream of the promised land of justice and freedom from oppression. The biblical metaphors travel through the centuries, enlivened by the prayers of all who rely on God's mercy in times of brokenness.

Like the ferries that ply Puget Sound, such images carry us from shore to shore. Risk is a real part of many decisions, and we can never be certain of outcomes in advance. As Paul reminds us in his letter to the Romans, we hope for what we cannot yet see (8:25). Hopeful imagination spans the distance between results not fully calculable beforehand and the action we must take. We make our way tentatively between the old and the new. As a family prepares to move to another part of the country, they must say good-bye to familiar streets and stores, friends, classmates, and coworkers. Their new location feels foreign and frightening. Will they find a house they can afford? Will there be good schools for the kids? Will they be able to make friends?

What if they don't like it? Suspended between old ways of being—even previous ways of experiencing God—and their new life, they must trust that good things await them. They make this goodness more likely by envisioning together the new life they want to create for themselves. The hopeful images of exodus and exile tell them that God will be with them, providing the strength they need along the way. Just so did the Israelites trust in the *Shekinah*, or divine presence, to accompany them on their journey, especially in difficult times.

Remembering Who God Is for Us and Who We Can Be

In her novel *Adam Bede*, George Eliot beautifully describes how we need past touchstones in order to believe we can survive yet again: "There is no despair so absolute as that which comes with the first moments of our first great sorrow, when we have not yet known what it is to have suffered and be healed, to have despaired and recovered hope." For a child, disappointment fills the whole screen and pain promises to be everlasting. But experience tells us that darkness does lift, and grace arrives. Since we have made it through similar crises in the past, perhaps we can do so again.

As the poets of Israel knew, memory alleviates fear by assuring us that we have survived similar situations. When the Israelites renewed their covenant, it was accompanied by a ceremony in which they recalled how God had blessed and saved them by bringing them out of Egypt and protecting them on their journeys (Josh. 24:16ff). This remembering did not simply mark past events; it defined present possibilities. The gospels likewise ask us to remember who God is for us and therefore who we can be. As Jesus eats his final meal with his disciples, he tells them to eat and drink again in memory of him. This meal will serve as a ritual of remembrance, reenacting the dying and rising that he is about to undertake. In the darkest of nights, his disciples are to draw hope from his Passover. It defines the core of Christian life, and we enter into it each time we let go and lose our lives only to find them given to us again by God.

Several spiritual practices support the kind of remembering that revives hope. These prayer forms remind us, lest we forget, who God is and has been for us. They call to mind the grace hidden in our personal history as well as in the entire cosmos. Sufism, the mystical path of Islam, incorporates such a special kind of remembrance into prayer.

Memory alleviates fear by assuring us that we have survived similar situations.

It includes rites based on the importance the Quran gives not just to the supreme name of God as Allah but also to God's other "most beautiful Names" (7:180). Tradition considers the number of these names to be ninety-nine. My husband and I have a framed parchment from Egypt containing these divine names in Arabic script. A friend gave it to us with the stipulation that we regard both it and the names it contains with reverence.

All Muslims are to remember that the entire universe reflects, in a variety of combinations, the harmony and contrasts found in this galaxy of divine names. The ultimate quest of Islam, as the Quran characterizes it, is to seek "the Face of God" (2:115). But the Sufis place special emphasis on remembering God by mentioning these names. This practice, known as *dhikr*, has taken different forms—for example, rhythmic repetition of words and phrases from the Quran, silent forms of inner meditation, or ecstatic dancing to flutes and drums.

Some of these names for God are the Just, the Majestic, the Reckoner, the Giver of Death, the Victorious, and the All-Powerful; also the All-Merciful, the Forgiver, the Gentle, the Generous, the Beautiful, and Love. The Muslim's religious life moves rhythmically between these paradoxical poles of the Divine: far beyond our reach yet dwelling within the hearts of the faithful; judging with justice but forgiving with mercy; punishing the wicked but loving and forgiving all creatures. No matter what one has done, a Muslim should never despair of God's compassion and mercy (39:53). This hopeful trust is expressed in the prayer of an Islamic woman, reported by Seyyed Hossein Nasr: "O Lord, have Mercy and Compassion, for if Thou does not have Mercy, who will have mercy?" As the Quran states, "Surely God's friends—no fear shall be on them, neither shall they sorrow" (10:63).

The practices found in Jewish, Christian, and Islamic traditions of reviving hope by remembrance alert us to the personal history of grace contained in each life story. We are frequently more fully aware of our history of sorrow and pain than of our history of joy and hope, but prayer practices can make our graced past available to us as well. These practices fit most helpfully into our spiritual journey after we have had time to heal painful memories and mourn our losses and sorrows in the full-throated way of the biblical Psalms: "See, O Lord, how distressed I am; my stomach churns, my heart is wrung within me" (Lam. 1:20); "The thought of my affliction and my homelessness is wormwood and gall! My soul continually thinks of

Prayer practices can make our graced past available to us.

it and is bowed down within me" (Lam. 3:19–20). The next verses of this lament show us grief giving way to hope: "But this I call to mind and therefore I have hope: The steadfast love of the Lord never ceases" (Lam. 3:21–22). Sorrow and gratitude lie close together—as a suffering patient knows when nursing aides change the sheets and prop up fresh pillows around him. After mourning has cleared a space, gratitude and hope can arise.

Litanies, a way of prayer that arose in the fourth century from the prayer of the laity in Eastern Christianity, can then be used to recall and celebrate God's beauty, creativity, and strength in our personal stories. Litany takes a variety of forms. One method, the naming of past graces and victories, grounds reasons for present hope.

You might create a litany for yourself that goes something like this one, but that mentions specific details from your own life:

Creator God,
Grant me the gift of remembering.
Let me not forget your faithful care,
your sustenance in days of despair,
how you upheld me until I saw the sun
    dawn yet again.
Blessed are you.

I will not cease to remember how my mourning
    turned to laughter, my loneliness opened into
    friendship, and
my brokenness issued in courage.
Blessed are you.

Help me recall your presence at my side
when I leapt into the unknown and landed safely,
when I said yes to love, a new job, forgiveness,
when I set out for vistas not yet explored.
Blessed are you.

May I not miss your Spirit deep within all my
    seasons—blossom of desert, bounty of harvest,
    white rush of winter beauty, verdant breeze of
    springtime.
Blessed are you.

Bring to mind my past faithfulness, victories,
    endurance, breakthroughs, and joy.
Let these brace my hope now.
Blessed are you.
Keep me ever mindful of your faithful love.
Amen.

You can add to this litany a simple ritual that symbolizes your hope. Have near you, as you begin, an empty vase and seasonal flowers. As you mention each hope-filled memory, place a flower in the vase. In the end, you will have a visible reminder of the Spirit's movement in your personal history.

Letting Stories of Faith Change Our Perspective

Reflection on imagination and memory has shown that many kinds of stories nurture hope. My husband Tom recently had an experience of this power of story to shape the lens through which we see the world. A thunder and lightning storm struck during an afternoon visit with one of his friends, prompting her to reflect on similar storms when she was growing up. Her childhood home stood on an acreage with empty fields, allowing a clear view of the horizon as it met the land. Whenever a storm blew in, her mother would gather all the kids in front of the largest living room window. Like a movie screen, it framed the spectacle outside. There she taught them about the marvels and the awe-inspiring power of nature. They learned to respect and wonder at its mystery. When storms come now in this friend's neighborhood, she rushes to the window to watch. She has learned to love, not fear, the storms of life.

This account surprised Tom. His childhood memory of electric storms in Wisconsin differed greatly. He would often awake to find his mother lighting candles throughout the house while murmuring prayers to the saints for protection from the terrifying elements. The family huddled in fear in the dark. Storms evoke these memories for him even today.

Both hope and fear reside within a circle of stories. Like the differing responses Tom and his friend have to electrical storms, we find within our own history the origins of many of our current ways of being in the world. Most cultures add to these personal stories a treasury of myths, fables, and other tales that shape the common spirit. These stories show us how to order and structure life; they offer blueprints for action and are a means of passing wisdom to succeeding generations. Like J.R.R. Tolkien's *The Lord of the Rings*, they frequently chronicle the perennial struggle between good and evil, the suffering and wounds that afflict us, and the hopeful outcomes possible for those who live with faith and love. Such overarching narratives enable us to vicariously face fear—and even emerge at the story's end more hopeful and courageous. These primary narratives share the goal of every belief system: to make sense of a creation in which we must suffer and ultimately die. The faith stories we tell ourselves help to confront this fear at its deepest level.

> *Both hope and fear reside within a circle of stories.*

However, truly turning such a narrative into a lens for seeing life requires more than simply listening in a detached and casual way. We need to become participants, not merely observers, of the stories. Their words must enter into our marrow. An ancient method of prayer presents such a way to access our most powerful faith stories. Rather than analyzing their words, we allow the accounts to *read us*.

This prayer, practiced by both monks and laypeople in the early Christian centuries, is called Lectio Divina (literally, "divine reading"). It dates to the beginnings of monasticism, reaching back to the sixth century and the Rule of St. Benedict. Lectio helps us truly hear biblical stories in a way that transforms us. Further, everyone, old and young, individuals and groups, can pray this way. It works well as family prayer, especially in sad or frightening times.

Lectio is a way of listening to scripture at ever deeper levels of attention. It offers a helpful path when we are too anxious and scattered for centering prayer. The passage itself engages mind and heart, distracting us at least momentarily from the worries that fill our consciousness. Through a simple process, Lectio also opens us to contemplation, or resting in God.

Whether done alone or in a group setting, the basic flow of this prayer remains the same. Think of its movement as a spiral circling you back to the same passage again and again but each time in a new way. For community or family prayer, you might begin the prayer time by lighting a candle and sitting in a circle.

The next steps need not be followed rigidly, since at times you may be moved more directly to any of Lectio's dimensions.

- *Select a passage from scripture.* Any passage can be used for Lectio. Begin with a section you love, or one that has touched you in the past. For example, try reading Luke 12:22–31, which reassures us that God cares for us no less than for the birds of the air or the lilies of the field:

"Consider the ravens; they neither sow nor reap, they have neither storehouse nor barn, and yet God feeds them. Of how much more value are you than the birds! And can any of you by worrying add a single hour to your span of life?" (12:24–25).

- *Slowly read the passage.* The emphasis here is on hearing the Word, on listening rather than analyzing. Let the passage gather you in. Enter into its rhythm. This is not speed-reading; make room for pauses and silences. You might think of it as the passage reading and interpreting you, rather than your interpreting it.

- *Meditate on the words.* Stop and reflect in silence on any sections that move you. If in a group, after some moments of silence you might share responses to the passage ("I hear God calling me to greater trust"; "The statement 'And can any of you by worrying add a single hour to your span of life?' challenges me more powerfully than ever before to let go of my concern with how long I have to live").

- *Express any prayers that arise in you.* What touches your mind and heart? What prayers are you moved to say? If you are with a group, share any of them you wish ("O God, help me to see that you will care for me no matter what happens"; "Thank you, O God, that you hold even the smallest aspects of creation in your loving hands").

- *Rest in the silent presence of God.* The final movement of this prayer invites us to simply *be* for a time in God's presence, whether alone or with others.

- *Close with a prayer or hymn if you wish.* Choose a familiar prayer to end your sessions. Some also find it helpful to record their prayer experience in a journal, or select a word or phrase from it to accompany them during the day.

Many passages can be prayed to deepen in us the hopeful core of the Hebrew and Christian Scriptures: Isaiah's consoling yet challenging word to his people in exile (43:1–23); Jacob's nocturnal struggle with an angel from which he emerges wounded but blessed by God (Gen. 32:22–32); the account of Jesus' cure of the bent-over woman who stands up tall again (Luke 13:10–17); or his encounter with a woman suffering from an incurable flow of blood whose hemorrhaging finally stops (Mark 5:25–34). If scripture is not a part of your life at this time, try Lectio with another religious text that does speak to you, such as poetry or a favorite work of fiction.

Praying stories of faith, along with imagining and remembering, revives hope. When we are tempted to let anxiety completely color the future, these practices release alternate possibilities. They teach us how to open to God's greening, to walk with the Spirit in desolate times.

Chapter Seven

The Love That Casts out Fear

If we work together, pray, and stand together, we can
create a new heaven and ease life for each other.
—THEA BOWMAN

A HASIDIC TALE tells of a deaf man who one evening
passes a house where a grand party is taking place. A
wedding festival fills the household with joy. Musicians play
upon their instruments, and the guests merrily dance to the
music. But the man looking through the window sees only
people whirling around the room, leaping and throwing their
arms in strange gestures. "How they fling themselves about!"
he exclaims. He concludes that the partygoers have gone
mad, for he cannot hear the music to which they are dancing.

In a violent world, relying on love as a solution to
fear likewise appears to be madness. To those who cannot
hear its music, love looks simply weak and sentimental, a
David facing the Goliath of modern dangers. From the time
human beings encountered saber-toothed tigers and poison-
ous snakes, fear has counseled pitched battle or quick exit,
and we continue to view fight or flight as the best guarantee

of safety. In contemporary terms, this translates into endless warfare or gated communities.

Yet a nearly universal tenet among spiritual traditions proposes another way. It designates love as the only reliable route to the security we so desperately seek. Many spiritual paths understand love as the very nature and being of God, and the only force powerful enough to truly overcome fear. How are we to understand this essential connection between fear and love? Along with the joy of being alive, the survival of our planet depends on the answer.

> *Love is the only reliable route to the security we so desperately seek.*

Knowing We Are Loved and Valued

Whenever we feel anxious, eliminating the external threat to our well-being looks like the formula for peace. Get a new job with fewer critical colleagues. Move to a part of town without crime. Be more suspicious of strangers. Buy a bigger car for road safety. It doesn't usually occur to us to examine our own heart for clues to relief. Yet many research studies establish the fact that what most powerfully serves as a buffer against anxiety is not changing external circumstances but increasing our own sense of self-worth. High self-esteem reduces anxiety, and low self-esteem increases it. An abiding sense of our own value affords the most fundamental sense of security.

My experience as a therapist confirms these research results. An accomplished teacher agonizes endlessly over her classes, sure that her past success was a fluke and she will be exposed as the fraud she is. An attractive, articulate man fears no woman could be interested in him, and so he spends his days alone and depressed. Perpetual anxiety hovers around a perception of not being smart, thin, talented, successful, or holy enough. So many gifts are blocked and buried by anxiety about not measuring up, as though our lives were held in a painful vise rather than the hands of a compassionate Creator.

Even when unacknowledged, such questioning of our worth remains potent. A common psychological mechanism takes the fears we conceal from ourselves and turns them out onto others. Melissa West describes this process in *If Only I Were a Better Mother.* She terms those parts of herself that she hides from others—her anger, jealousy, loneliness, and fear—the *dark mother.* West believes these emotions become dangerous precisely because we keep them out of sight. Poured out onto others, they turn into blame and prejudice. Hidden within us, they morph into depression or resentment.

A Taoist parable makes this point well. In the story of the Stolen Ax, a woodcutter sets out one morning to cut some firewood. When he discovers that his favorite ax is missing, he searches frantically for it in his shed, behind his house, and around the woodpile. He cannot find it anywhere, and he becomes more and more agitated. Suddenly he spies his neighbor's son out of the corner of his eye.

"Look at him shifting nervously there near the woodshed," he thinks. "What a guilty look he has on his face. I won't be able to prove it, but I'm certain he stole my ax!" The wood-cutter determines to get even for the crime. The next day he stumbles on the ax lying next to the firewood and realizes it is right where he left it when he was done splitting wood. When the woodcutter next sees the neighbor's son, he thinks, *How odd, somehow between yesterday and today that boy has lost his guilty look.* As in this tale from China, our own fears and hungers color how we see everything.

In the grip of fear, human beings put others into categories that are sweeping and dangerously ill informed. These groupings flow from generalizations on race, religion, gender, national origin, and the like; they create a climate of intolerance and hatred. Moreover, once this fear gets converted to anger as a shield against more vulnerable feelings, it can lead to blind destruction as a way of producing a perception of safety. Those who live with a sense of their own value are most able to move beyond such intolerance and operate out of love rather than hatred or fear.

In the grip of fear, human beings put others into categories that are sweeping and dangerously ill informed.

The link between self-worth and tolerance explains why the injunction to love oneself is at the core of so many spiritual traditions. The conviction that we are loved empowers us to love ourselves, which allays the insecurity we so often feel. This frees us to see, with the fifteenth-century Christian mystic Nicholas of Cusa, that God is the Face of faces present in all faces, though hidden as if in a riddle: "Thou art my image and the image of everyone, in such a way that Thou art our truth."

So how do we learn to love and value ourselves? This constitutes a lifetime's work of grace and personal courage. But the key is this: we have to start taking in the love of God and the love of others. The spiritual life begins with acceptance of God's love. Too often the bible passages that cling to us from childhood deliver messages of judgment and punishment. We must try instead to spend time with sections that deepen our awareness of God's unlimited love for us, even in the midst of our awkward, failed attempts at goodness. It helps to just let the words linger, circulating in mind and spirit as we go about the day.

> *Do not fear, for I have redeemed you;*
> *I have called you by name, you are mine.*
> *When you pass through the waters, I will be*
> *   with you;*
> *and through the rivers, they shall not*
> *   overwhelm you;*
> *when you walk through fire you shall not be*
> *   burned,*
> *and the flames shall not consume you. . . .*
> *Because you are precious in my sight, and honored,*
> *and I love you.*
>
> —ISAIAH 43:1–2, 4

101

Beloved, let us love one another, because love is
    from God;
everyone who loves is born of God and knows God.
Whoever does not love does not know God, for God
    is love.

    —1 John 4:7

As you hold these sayings in your heart, try to notice where you need to let yourself be loved—the place where you may be blocking the love already offered you. For example, instead of turning away a compliment, take it in and say thank you. See the fresh fruit of summer, the splendor of autumn leaves, the vast ocean—all of creation—as God's loving gift to you. Notice a smile or warm greeting, the outreach of a friend, the kind words of a family member. Learn to soak up love like a sponge, or a face lifted to the sun. It may take time, but gradually allowing yourself to accept love alters how you see yourself and others.

Sheltered by Others

Perhaps your memory of handling fear resembles what some of my clients describe as the "buck up" philosophy of life. Growing up, they were exhorted to hold their head high and carry on in spite of what scared them. Boys especially were told never to admit to being afraid. To do so invited ridicule, bullying, or worse. But this Lone Ranger model of dealing with fear no longer claims widespread allegiance. It is increasingly clear that close connection with other people, and not isolated stoicism, furnishes the most basic and enduring protection against fear.

Nearly 90 percent of stress research has been done on men. But as studies incorporate women's experience as well as men's, new insights emerge about gender differences in response to fear. In *The Tending Instinct,* Shelley E. Taylor reports the results of a UCLA study that reveals how women deal with tumultuous emotions such as fear. Previously, scientists believed that stress triggers hormones that prepare the body to stand up and fight or quickly flee. This ancient survival response enabled our ancestors to confront immediate danger in their environment. But the UCLA study

In response to fear women nurture one another.

suggests that women have a wider repertoire of responses to fear than simply fight or flight. In fact, they characteristically handle stress by making and strengthening friendships with other women. A hormone called *oxytocin,* released as part of the stress response, leads a woman to tend children and gather with other women. When she does this, even more oxytocin is released, and it in turn has a calming effect. In other words, in response to fear women nurture one another. This tending and befriending heals and prolongs lives. It also brings joy.

A well-known example of this is a 1989 study by Stanford psychiatrist David Spiegel. He formed support groups of women with advanced breast cancer who were not expected to survive for long. These terminally ill patients participated in small groups of about fifteen women. The women attended the groups for about an hour and a half each week for more than a year. Their conversations, facilitated by a psychiatrist or social worker, ranged over a variety of topics: how to handle the side effects of treatment, the impact of the cancer on their lives, how to be more assertive with doctors, the way in which the cancer helped them find meaning in their lives, their feelings of isolation and loss. The results were dramatic and unexpected. The women in the groups lived twice as long as those who did not participate—on average nearly a year and a half longer.

One reason this warm companionship may have extended the women's lives is that talking with others left them less anxious and depressed. They also felt cared for and affirmed, which raises self-esteem. These women's increased inner peace reduced adverse effects on the immune system and slowed the progress of the illness.

Our stress systems react less strongly if supportive people are with us, and when already engaged, these systems return to normal more quickly in the presence of such people. Family and friends—and sometimes strangers as well—calm anxiety. With them we can talk over our fears of surviving after a divorce or making the plunge to get married, of confronting a boss or taking a new career path, of facing family conflict or giving a public presentation.

In her influential study *Trauma and Recovery*, Judith Herman adds her own witness to the power of love in overcoming fear. Her book represents the fruit of two decades of clinical work with victims of violence, as well as extensive research on the experience of traumatized people, from combat veterans to survivors of political terror. In her research, Herman noticed that survivors' testimonies repeatedly mentioned moments when their sense of connection was restored by another person's act of generosity. This care reawakened something the survivor believed to be lost forever—faith, courage, compassion—and enabled the person to reclaim it. She recounts the story of a group of prisoners liberated from a Nazi concentration camp. Three of the prisoners had repaired a broken window and stove. As the stove began to spread its heat, another prisoner proposed that everyone offer a slice of bread to the three who had been working on their behalf. They agreed to do so. This mutual exchange of care marked the moment when the prisoners began to reclaim their humanity.

Herman believes human connection plays a central role in healing the most intense kind of fear, terror: "The solidarity of a group provides the strongest protection against terror and despair, and the strongest antidote to traumatic experience." People who survive trauma learn that their sense of self, worth, and humanity depends on a feeling of connection to others. Whereas the trauma they endured isolated and degraded them, community offers acceptance, affirmation, and a sense of belonging.

Even when the traditional fight or flight, rather than "tend and befriend," is considered the main response to fear, current neuroscience finds that calm words and caring physical contact decrease fear. Science explains this as the limbic system's powerful reaction to a personal human presence and the sound of the human voice. Described in technical terms, this means that human connection decreases the fight-or-flight response of the sympathetic nervous system and increases the "rest-and-digest" pattern of the parasympathetic nervous system. In fact, our earliest ancestors survived only through cooperation.

There are indications that men as well as women enjoy a more varied response to fear. In military combat, a phenomenon known as bunching has been noted. A commander describes how the men in the field "bunch and hunch. . . . Try as I will to get my fifty spaced out, they must creep back for the comforting assurance weaned from close companionship." From an even earlier disaster comes evidence of male contact in times of terror. When Mount Vesuvius erupted in A.D. 79, thousands of residents in the city of Pompeii on the Bay of Naples died before they could escape. They were engulfed by a series of intense surge clouds. Buried under tons of superheated ash, the city is preserved just as it was at the moment of its destruction. In a house on the main street of Pompeii, a father and his son, estimated to be about fourteen, died instantly. The boy is on his back, gazing up at his father. The two are holding hands.

Love does indeed cast out fear. In good times and bad, we are tethered to one another. What would happen if all human beings, men as well as women, developed a broader repertoire of responses to fear? Might we know greater intimacy in our friendships, better cooperation at work, closer ties with family members? Might we have less violence and war, and no longer feel compelled to go to battle to deal with forms of stress such as fear?

Perfect Strangers

In the second century, a plague struck the cities and towns of the Roman Empire, killing a third to a half of the population. As the deadly virus swept through Asia Minor, Italy, and Gaul, people fled. But some of the early Christians stayed to care for the sick and dying. They professed a God of love who asked love in return. Jesus, their leader, gathered Jewish tradition into his own teaching by telling his followers to love God with their whole heart, mind, and soul and their neighbor as themselves (Mark 12:28–31).

The followers of Jesus loved their way out of fear. Even small actions on behalf of others reduce fear. These expressions of compassion lift the helplessness and hopelessness that accompany anxiety. As Jesus' disciples pushed past fear, they drew from a well of faith deeper than surface turmoil. Their courage arose from the

In the action of loving we live in God and experience God living in us.

conviction that the divine is love itself, and so in the action of loving we live in God and experience God living in us. Such faith generates unparalleled boldness. What else matters? What can really harm us? The conclusion follows: "There is no fear in love, but perfect love casts out fear" (1 John 4:18).

I worked for some years in a nursing center and saw in a practical setting how love propelled people past their fears. Many relatives of residents dreaded setting foot in a nursing home. Sons and daughters would sheepishly admit to me that they could barely bring themselves to visit their parents. The sight of disability, loneliness, decline, and death—their own personal Everest—seemed too daunting. The way past the fear was actually to spend more time with a loved one in this environment, rather than to avoid coming. Then the residents ceased to be defined by external appearance and emerged as interesting and complex human beings.

Compassionate actions seed hope in a community. This happens especially when a shared disaster such as an earthquake or flood reveals our common vulnerability. The buffer against fear often consists of unpretentious acts of kindness. On Christmas Eve of 2003, my sister and I were waiting for a bus to take us to downtown Seattle. Dire headlines screamed from the newspapers that morning. The terror alert had been raised to orange, and Air France flights to the United States were cancelled because of hijacking fears. A case of mad cow disease was discovered in our state. A possible new SARS outbreak was being investigated in China. Meanwhile, on the street, more immediate concerns prevailed. A bus lift jammed while lowering a woman in her wheelchair. She hung suspended on the lift, unable to get off or get back on. Anxiety lined her face. When it became clear that neither she nor the bus was going anywhere for the moment, and that the problem would have to await the arrival of a mechanic, the other passengers began to wander off the bus. Then surprising things started to happen. One passenger returned with a take-out lunch and handed it to the stranded woman. A man who clearly had very limited means himself offered her his bus pass. The graciousness of strangers lessened the woman's helplessness, as well as their own, and somehow buoyed my sister and me amid the larger dangers to our global community.

A late fourteenth-century mystic, Julian of Norwich made the link between love and well-being the cornerstone of her writing. Her era was a time of upheaval not unlike our own. Anxiety permeated Europe as the Black Plague claimed ever more victims and the Hundred Years' War raged. The church wallowed in corruption, its authority weakened by a long, drawn-out papal election.

Julian dedicated her life to prayer and reflection from her hermitage in England, her cat and garden her main companions. There, at the age of thirty, she received the revelations that fed her theology. One of the most powerful showed her the range and depth of God's love and goodness. God created and redeemed us out of love and longs to be united with us in the end. The worst that can happen to us—suffering and sin—has been transfigured by Christ's passion and resurrection. Her best-known saying spoke directly to the darkness and fear of her age, and it continues to inspire ours: "All will be well, and all will be well, and every kind of thing will be well."

Chapter Eight

The Core of Courage

There is a spirit that pervades everything, that is capable of powerful song and radiant movement, and that moves in and out of the mind. The colors of this spirit are multitudinous, a glowing, pulsing rainbow.

—PAULA GUNN ALLEN

S OME YEARS AGO, while having lunch at the nursing center where I worked, I looked up just as one of our newest residents reached the end of the cafeteria line. Balancing his lunch tray with its assorted selections, Tony stopped to survey the large dining room filled with tables of strangers. Watching him, I recalled the many recent upheavals in his life. He and his wife were longtime residents of an Italian neighborhood in New York City. Then one night she suffered a massive stroke that completely changed their lives. Tony had to sell their home of forty years and move to the West Coast to be near the couple's only daughter. Now his wife lay speechless and immobile in a nursing home, and he lived in a nearby retirement apartment. As Tony paused, I saw fear flicker briefly across his face. Then he drew back his shoulders, moved to a nearby

111

table, and asked to join the group for lunch. Tony's quiet courage moved me deeply.

During more than two decades as a therapist and spiritual director, I have often witnessed the courage of ordinary people. A recently widowed woman forces herself to get out of bed in the morning, although she dreads the waves of emptiness and longing she knows will sweep over her. An adult son initiates a conversation with his father whose anger terrified him as a child, and he finds that he can now hold his own. People change careers, speak up in class, stand up for causes, get married, raise children, and walk with dying friends even though they are scared. Grace upholds them in ways they could not envision, and in the process they discover spiritual resources they do not believe they possess.

What we most want for ourselves is moral courage, the virtue by which we act with integrity in spite of fear.

Courage enables us to brave dangers and move through obstacles, endure suffering or lift ourselves out of it. It may benefit self, or save another from peril or even death. Although we admire physical courage—extreme sports, athletic feats, daring adventures—what we most want for ourselves is that quality of spirit called *moral courage*, the virtue by which we act with integrity in spite of fear. Moral courage reveals us at our best, and it calls to those depths in us desirous of such graced humanity.

No single definition captures the complex reality we call *courage*. It turns out to be more like a mosaic than a single stone, with diverse elements contributing to its composition. It is a diamond whose multiple facets become visible only when examined from many angles. Courage involves vulnerability, faith, love, honesty, empathy, wisdom, endurance, and trust. Taken together, these components reveal the core meaning of *courage*. Contemplating them can renew our own courage and expand its place in our spiritual lives.

Awareness of Our Vulnerability

It may seem strange to begin a discussion of courage with a term like *vulnerability*, which calls to mind weakness rather than strength. But courage is not the absence of fear, or the pretense that we are totally adequate and impervious to threat. I remember a friend, a survivor of domestic violence herself, who was asked to give a talk on violence against women. She agreed to do it and then found herself filled with dread. What was this resistance? She went to a place of quiet and let the fear come in, asking what it looked like and what it said to her. She discovered that what fed the fear was her sense that she was too emotional, unhealed, and lacking in professional credentials to dare address the issue. After praying about it, she decided to deal with these insecurities head on and go forward with the talk.

Creative action always includes the risk of failure. If we are unwilling to fail, we will have to avoid many precarious things: marriage, having children, settling conflict, working for justice. Courage is often stitched together from those moments when we wish we had possessed it and instead found ourselves wanting. We know well the fragility of all we love and hold dear, including life itself. Courage does not demand that we deny this awareness.

Paradoxically, fear and courage coexist. In fact, the people who are most vulnerable—the sick or poor, citizens of a war-torn region, those living under a dictator—often exhibit the most extraordinary courage. Courage manifests the gospel paradox of finding strength in weakness, and life in death: "But we have this treasure in clay jars, so that it may be made clear that this extraordinary power belongs to God and does not come from us" (2 Cor. 4:7). New Testament images of jewels hidden in clay pots, marvelous plants emerging from buried seeds, and ordinary faces harboring glory suggest that acknowledging fear, grief, and death simultaneously nurtures hope and courage. Faith is a way to grapple with vulnerability.

In *Fear and Other Uninvited Guests*, Harriet Lerner describes how this spiritual truth about acknowledging insecurity makes psychological sense. She names an essential aspect of bravery: "You have to keep showing up!" Lerner uses her own fear of flying as an example. No amount of information could convince her that when she flew the plane would not crash and leave her children orphans. What finally helped her was taking action. She bought airline tickets and flew. Finally, she says, she had to fly so often that her fear disappeared: "Experience gave me comfort where reasoning had failed." If we have a real phobia or panic disorder, it is important to get treatment. Otherwise, what we need, Lerner believes, is more experience with the activity we dread. Avoiding an activity such as public speaking, a dinner party, or a family gathering simply increases the conviction that the threat is real. The fears we evade shrink our heart and mind.

In contrast, recognizing our vulnerability without succumbing to it results in inner peace and a sense of personal integrity. In *Strength in Weakness*, her collection of writings by eighteenth-century Quaker women, Gil Skidmore notes that choices for courage pervade their lives in small, quiet ways—and the gift of peace follows. Skidmore relates how a Quaker woman named Mary Alexander had a strong call to speak at a prayer meeting but failed to do so. This failure left her in great distress of mind, and she prayed for another chance to remedy it. It came at the next meeting, after a friend spoke: "As soon as he sat down, I stood up and began with the before-mentioned petition: 'Thou hast given me a south land; give me also springs of water,' and after commenting a little upon it, I sat down *full of peace*."

It is hard to face our own fragility, and the limits of existence itself, without falling into discouragement or despair. These limits take us into dark corners of the heart. The twentieth-century theologian Paul Tillich recognized this dilemma, defining faith as the courage to accept acceptance. In *The Courage to Be*, Tillich says that courage becomes possible once we make the final act of trust. We accept the fact that God loves us, and this enables us to be ourselves even when faced with the threat of emptiness, condemnation, or death. The gift of being accepted by God, just as we are, frees us from anxiety. In fact, he considers the very possibility of courage to be rooted in this grace of ultimate trust in God.

Knowing What We Love and Value

Tucked inside the word *courage* lies *cor*, the Latin designation for heart. Courage involves honoring commitment and living from conviction, even if we are afraid. In fact, the only thing powerful enough to overcome fear is a goal fed by the heart's desires. Since courage draws upon the heart's resources, it matters what shape our heart is in. What will we discover in that deepest core of the self when we are frightened and still must do the right thing? Will the center hold? The answer lies not so much in trying to pump up our moral muscles as in becoming clear about what we love and believe and integrating those values more fully into our lives. Whom and what do I love?

Courage follows from the sense of what really matters and in turn reinforces it.

What does that love ask of me? Courage follows from this sense of what really matters and in turn reinforces it.

A story of bravery on behalf of nature illustrates how such habitual honoring of one's truth stands up when tested. In 1962 Rachel Carson published *Silent Spring,* one of the most influential and controversial books on the environment ever written. In it she documented the alarming consequences of widespread and indiscriminate pesticide use. Drawing on her fourteen years in the Fish and Wildlife

Service, Carson exposed loopholes in federal environmental regulation and efforts to cover up pesticide hazards. Her meticulous research revealed widespread wildlife death, fish kills, the looming threat of cancer, collusion between academic science and industry, and the silence of the medical profession. Carson selected only the most substantiated examples and painstakingly checked the accuracy of her findings. She knew the book's foundation had to be unshakable to withstand the storm it would engender.

The pesticide industry immediately waged war against Carson and her book, first trying to prevent publication and then withdrawing financial support from media outlets that reviewed it positively. Corporate scientists ridiculed and undermined the book, even claiming it would bring about famine and death. Though Carson was a technically trained scientist writing with scientific rigor, critics charged that *Silent Spring* was too poetic and called it soft science.

In spite of the aggressive crusade waged against it, *Silent Spring* stirred the world. Subsequent hearings on the environment led to formation of the Environmental Protection Agency and development of legal grounds for banning DDT. Every country in which it was widely read held hearings on environmental legislation. In April 1970, Earth Day was celebrated. Even cartoons portrayed the book's impact; a grasshopper prays, "God bless Momma and Poppa . . . and Rachel Carson."

How did Carson summon the courage to take on so many formidable opponents? She did not set out to be a heroine. In fact when she first became aware of the problems created by the new kinds of pesticides, Carson tried to get others to write about them. A private, modest person, she did not seek the spotlight. Nor did she intend to start an ecological revolution. In her acknowledgments for *Silent Spring,* she says she knew she had to write the book when a friend's letter pulled her attention back to issues that had long concerned her. Troubled by the threat to the web of life, she refused to turn away from the truth. Instead, she dedicated her talents to making the message known. As she completed her book, Carson wrote to her friend Dorothy Freeman that she would be unable to happily listen to the song of a thrush if she had not done all she could to prevent this assault on all the birds and other creatures, all the loveliness of nature.

Each time we refuse to betray our most important values, each time we face down a fear that tells us we cannot do what we must, strength grows.

We cannot know with certainty if our courage will hold up as Carson's did when it was tested. But we can take the small steps that gradually make us courageous. Each time we refuse to betray our most important values, each time we face down a fear that tells us we cannot do what we must, strength grows. Unlimited opportunities for courage occur every day. The person who can bring herself to undertake a nonviolent protest for peace may struggle to confront difficult issues with a roommate. No matter. We walk the path of courage we can manage at any given time, a journey with God's Spirit, largely hidden from others' view.

The Capacity for Empathy

The major religious traditions—Indigenous, Confucian, Hindu, Buddhist, Jewish, Christian, and Islamic—all agree on the importance of compassion. Though described in different ways, the ability to empathize with the other, to enter into that person's experience, is a key sign of spiritual life. We are to walk in another person's moccasins for a time, to realize the oneness of all beings, to recognize the similarity of all fears, suffering, and needs. Confucius summed up this golden rule in about 500 B.C.E.: "Do not do unto others what you would not have others do unto you." He taught his disciples to practice *shu*, "likening to oneself." This meant recognizing what gives us pain, and then refraining from inflicting similar suffering on others. Jesus makes such empathic love part of his greatest commandment: "You shall love your neighbor as yourself" (Mark 12:31).

Empathy inspires the courage to act on behalf of others. In *The Hand of Compassion*, Kristen Renwick Monroe profiles women and men who risked their lives to save Jews during World War II. She concentrates on only five among the many survivors and rescuers she interviewed: Margot, the daughter of a wealthy German, who moved to Holland, where she worked to save Jews in spite of being arrested several times; Otto, a German living in Czechoslovakia who joined the Austrian resistance movement and saved more than a hundred Jews before ending up in a concentration camp himself; John, a Dutchman who organized an escape network that took Jews to safety in Switzerland and Spain; Irene, a Polish nursing student who hid eighteen Jews in a home where she worked; and Knud, an inventor who helped with the rescue of 85 percent of the Jews in Denmark.

As Monroe listens to their stories, searching for insight into what drove them to engage in such acts of courage, she discovers that what most deeply motivated them was their sense that "we are all human beings." The value of caring for others was so deeply integrated that it became the underlying structure of their identity. They did not simply notice the suffering of the Jews; it became a moral imperative that required them to act. Margot describes the empathy that enabled her to cherish the humanity in others: "You don't walk away. You don't walk away from somebody who needs real help." In Otto's words: "The hand of compassion was faster than the calculus of reason." Their actions seemed to them to be the natural and automatic thing to do, even though they knew there were others who did in fact turn away. As Irene says: "I must take the right path, or I would no longer be myself."

Studies other than Monroe's reveal some of the same characteristics she found in people we would call heroes or heroines. Those who rush to aid someone trapped in a burning car, plunge into freezing waters, or scale mountains to rescue the injured cannot imagine acting otherwise. They do not think they are doing anything unusual. Anybody would do the same, they say. Asked where they found the courage to do what they did, they reply that it was the right thing to do, that they were raised to help someone who needs help, that what matters more than any material possessions is love of others. A young woman who saved a friend from drowning puts it this way: "For a second I was like, 'I gotta get out of here.' Then I thought, 'No, I can't leave my best friend out there to die.'" As with Monroe's subjects, these women and men extend their care beyond personal acquaintances to all human beings. One rescuer comments: "I have a sister; I have a mom who lives in that area. Even so, I would have done it for anybody." Another says: "If I didn't try to stop her and she killed somebody, I might as well have been driving that car."

In the New Testament we read that to lay down your life for a friend is the greatest gift. But to do it for a stranger is even greater. Without always giving a religious name to it, these courageous people exemplify the universal spiritual principle of compassion for all beings. Such acts have power to expand a community's spiritual horizons. Even those not called to the same risks find in these larger acts of compassion inspiration for their own daily courage.

Sometimes an act of mercy on behalf of others exacts the full price of discipleship. There are those in every age who offer their lives out of love for the poor and oppressed, who die trying to bring about justice and dignity. On December 2, 1980, North American churchwomen Maura Clarke, Ita Ford, Dorothy Kazel, and Jean Donovan were murdered in El Salvador. A small plaque marks the country road where they are buried: "Receive them Lord

> *They were willing to relinquish all they held dear if it meant that others could live with greater abundance.*

into your Kingdom." These women died like Jesus because they struggled as he did for others. They were willing to relinquish all they held dear, to share in his cross, if it meant that others could live with greater abundance. They did not seek death but met it with immense faith and courage. Their witness, like that of many others, lights the way for others who walk much less risky paths of courage.

The Spirit's Gifts of Wisdom and Endurance

Courage drinks from the gifts of the Spirit that flow freely through creation. In *The Sacred Hoop*, Paula Gunn Allen, a Laguna Pueblo/Sioux scholar, names this creative spirit who enabled her Native American people to endure into the present in spite of assaults on their being, and to thrive beyond bitterness and rage: "She is the Old Woman who tends the fires of life. She is the Old Woman Spider who weaves us together in a fabric of interconnection." These titles evoke the transcendent power, the intelligence, that pervades the earth and blesses and challenges all peoples.

In the Hebrew Scriptures, this divine Spirit is called *Sophia*, or Wisdom. Sophia pervades the cosmos, dwelling with all beings and ordering all things. She brings about a powerful connectedness and teaches the ways of justice and courage:

And if anyone loves righteousness,
her labors are virtues;
for she teaches self-control and prudence,
justice and courage;
nothing is more profitable for mortals than these.

—WISDOM OF SOLOMON 8:7

Sophia offers us the strength to hope against hope, to endure in spite of pain and struggle, to reshape the present configuration into a better one.

The New Testament reminds us repeatedly of the gifts poured forth by the Spirit. These graces come in such abundance that they tumble over one another in Paul's letter to the Galatians: "love, joy, peace, patience, kindness, generosity, faithfulness, gentleness, and self-control" (Gal. 5:22). When we find ourselves jaded or discouraged, cynical or depleted, it is to this torrent of the Spirit's refreshing waters that we turn. It nourishes many kinds of daily courage: caring for a loved one with a long-term illness, holding on day after day though we are tired of our obligations and commitments, hanging in there with the demands of raising a child, refusing to let ourselves plummet when we feel empty or down, calling for help when we are tempted to take the drink that will blot it all out again. The Spirit supports courage for the long haul.

In the thirteenth century, the philosopher and theologian Thomas Aquinas included courage, or fortitude, among the four cardinal virtues (the other three being prudence, justice, and temperance). The word *cardinal* comes from the Latin term for *hinge*; these virtues form the axis on

123

which the moral life turns. Viewing courage as a cardinal virtue names something we instinctively sense: we simply cannot get through life without it. It is not just an isolated spiritual quality; we need it to successfully cope with all the situations we confront. For this reason, the fourth-to-fifth-century Christian theologian Augustine of Hippo called courage "love readily enduring all for the sake of what is loved."

In their studies of grassroots whistleblowers and activists in the United States, Israel, and the former Czechoslovakia, Myron and Penina Glazer laud the courage of ordinary people who expend themselves in various causes. Though the subjects of their research do not usually face a life-threatening situation, their battles require a long-term investment of time and energy. When these courageous people proclaim the dangers of serious occupational and community situations such as hazardous waste sites or unsafe automobile designs, they must be ready to face criticism of their competence and integrity, isolation from one-time neighbors and coworkers, and even division within their own family. How do they overcome fear and intimidation? They turn their anger into an emotional resource, using its energy to fuel their action. They draw on faith in the justice of their cause, convinced that the price of inaction is greater than that of action. For some, religious beliefs become an explicit factor in their protest. A psychiatrist who exposed conditions at a county mental health facility in California explained that the requirements of Torah, for him the essence of true Judaism, left him no choice:

"There is a saying in the Talmud that 'He who saves one life saves the whole world.'" This belief sustained the psychiatrist's actions, since he believed there was a strong likelihood that other people would die from the conditions he was protesting.

Meditations on Courageous Biblical Figures

Faithful courage defines many familiar biblical figures. Meditating on their lives concretizes our exploration of courage; it is a helpful way to deepen our own engagement with it. One form of such prayer is to listen imaginatively, in and through the biblical accounts, to what they might say in their own words about the wellspring of their courage.

The Prophet Jeremiah (1:1–19; 31:33): "I had a monumental sense of inadequacy. Mine may be one of the most public and problematic cases of performance anxiety you will ever see. When God said to me, 'Before I formed you in the womb I knew you, and before you were born I consecrated you; I appointed you a prophet to the nations,' I thought for sure it must be a case of mistaken identity. I pleaded: 'Ah, Lord God! Truly I do not know how to speak, for I am only a boy.' I had no gift for oratory, and yet I was being told to deliver a word of God that no one wanted to hear in the first place. The task had failure and ridicule written all over it. Everything in me rebelled against it. *Get someone else*, I thought.

"Yet God promised to be with me, to give me the words I needed. That made all the difference. God knew me better than I knew myself and saw layers of desire and potential talent I did not recognize. In truth, the word burned within me, ready for release. You probably know my story. All that my people of Israel had built up lay in ruins about us. Devastation and despair gripped us. We were hopeless and afraid. I was as frightened and in as much pain as anyone else. But with God's help, I was able to offer a message to my people, a word filled with both challenge and comfort. Yes, we had to change, but this was not the end of all we cherished.

"What I learned about courage is this: the grace comes when you need it, and it creates a highway through situations that appear impassable. Looking at events from the outside and ahead of time gives no indication of the strength that will be there in the actual doing of a deed. We can plead and beg internally to be spared, but trying to ignore the call simply does not work.

"Frankly, after being pushed by the divine I soared. The poetry was there when I needed it, and at times I couldn't believe my own Spirit-filled eloquence. On my lips, God's word came to life: 'But this is the covenant that I will make with the house of Israel after those days. I will put my law within them, and I will write it on their hearts; and I will be their God, and they shall be my people.' The message I delivered was clearly meant for all those in similar straits."

Mary of Nazareth (Luke 1:26–56): "Let me tell you what it is like to watch someone you love on a collision course with destruction. My son, Yeshua, walked just such a road. I saw the twisted faces of those who hated him, heard their agitated murmurs. I knew that it was only a matter of time before he would be killed. Yet he never veered from his mission. My own faith sometimes darkened, for I did not always understand my son's ministry or the ways of his God. It was my love for Yeshua, not a clear sense of what he was about, that enabled me to stand firmly with him even to the foot of his cross.

"To stay the course and follow him in what sometimes looked like folly, I had to burrow deeply into that Wisdom I trusted from the first announcement of Yeshua's birth. My courage floated then on the wings of the Spirit of God. I turned to that place in my heart when I saw the writing on the wall about his future.

"I remember how afraid I was when it became clear I would give birth. Because my pregnancy was outside the boundaries of law and custom, I knew I could be accused of adultery and stoned to death. As a young girl, I saw that happen to a woman, and the scene terrifies me even now. What reassured me was the angel's reminder: 'With God nothing will be impossible.'

"I needed support. I spent time with my cousin Elizabeth, a woman older and wiser in God's ways. I turned to my Jewish foremothers—Sarah, Rebecca, Miriam, Judith, Ruth. I wrapped their stories of passion, courage, and devotion around me like a cloak, drawing on its warmth and safety.

"I was no stranger to the ancient cruelties people visit on one another, but in my heart I also held the divine pledge of redemption: 'His mercy is for those who fear him from generation to generation.' Faith in this Mercy sustained me when my courage faltered. I was surprised over time to find myself turning into a bold and daring woman and disciple. I was ready to be both mother and sister to all who are urged by the same Spirit of God who strengthened me."

Chapter Nine

Courage and Fear as Contagious

We live our lives inscrutably included within the
streaming mutual life of the universe.
—MARTIN BUBER

IN DECEMBER 2004, Wangari Maathai became the first
woman from Africa to receive the Nobel Peace Prize.
The Nobel committee honored her conviction that peace
depends on our ability to sustain the Earth. Thirty years
ago, Maathai founded the Green Belt Movement, through
which she mobilized poor African women to plant thirty
million trees. Besides providing fuel, food, shelter, and
income for the women's families, the trees became symbols
of both the struggle for democracy in Kenya and peaceful
resolution of conflict.

The trees planted by members of Maathai's Green
Belt Movement witness to the way we seed courage in one
another. Emboldened by her leadership, the women of
Kenya brought about change tree by tree. They planted
them in Nairobi's Uhuru Park, at Freedom Corner, and in
other parts of the country to call for a peaceful transition to

democracy and the release of prisoners of conscience. They also used peace trees to settle disputes between communities.

In her Nobel acceptance speech, Maathai recalled her childhood experiences in rural Kenya. While growing up, she could visit a stream next to her house and gather water for her mother. She drank straight from its currents. With dismay she watched the river dry up as the forests were cleared and replaced by commercial plantations. One goal of her work is to return to children the beauty and wonder of nature she herself knew as a child. Maathai regards the healing of the Earth's wounds as intrinsic to healing our own. Concern for the Earth arises from the realization that we are part of a larger family of life. Convinced that the solution to global problems lies not outside us with our leaders but in our own commitment to justice, integrity, and trust, Maathai issues a spiritual challenge: "In the course of history, there comes a time when humanity is called to shift to a new level of consciousness, to reach a higher moral ground. A time when we have to shed our fear and give hope to each other. That time is now."

Maathai's work underscores how powerfully a person's fear or courage affects others. We often picture fear as a solitary possession, believing that whether we act with courage or cowardice pertains just to our own internal, spiritual struggle. But in fact both courage and fear are contagious, passed from person to person like a virus. Their social nature offers grounds for hope and despair alike, since emotions can either build up or tear apart the cosmic fabric.

By envisioning reality through a communal lens, seeing it as a tightly woven tapestry, we begin to understand how every thread brightens or diminishes the total configuration. Bringing a spiritual perspective to this interdependence assures us that we do not weave Creation's fabric alone. A Divine Artist works in and through our efforts to transmute

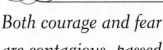

Both courage and fear are contagious, passed from person to person like a virus.

fear into courage. We find God's Spirit as the Depth and Ground of all living beings, the grace upholding fragile relationships. Scripture names God's creative activity in the world as the breath that enlivens us, the flowing waters that nourish us, the sheltering wings beneath which we find safety and joy. Exploring the spiritual implications of the social nature of fear and courage begins with understanding the kind of universe that binds us so closely together in God.

Fear and Courage in a Relational Universe

We do not often have the leisure to consider how we imagine the universe and our place in it. When we do so, we might discover that our image is of disparate individuals who somehow manage to connect at times, like the characters in the telephone ad who periodically reach out and touch one another. Or we might see ourselves woven tightly together with all other beings in a single web. Our perspective determines the basic assumptions of our spirituality, generating either a personal piety removed from the world's problems or a commitment to love the Earth and all who inhabit it.

Whether we advert to it or not, our view of the universe depends on the physics informing our consciousness. Many of us still live out of a Newtonian worldview, a science of separateness. Isaac Newton, whose physics determined how we see so many aspects of experience, thought that all objects in space and time, from atoms to astronauts, exist as discrete and independent individuals. His was a physics of disconnection, and though it is being replaced by a physics of relations it is still influential.

Science today presents a universe that is radically interconnected. In fact, our understanding of the field of matter-energy turns out to be just the opposite of what Newton thought. The universe is profoundly social; everything is implicated in everything else. Though its impact may be minimal, even the most distant constellation has effects on us, and we on it. This recognition of the interconnectedness of all things has given rise to the phrase "the butterfly effect." When a butterfly flutters its wings, it creates a tiny disturbance. If conditions are exactly right, this disturbance can be amplified and can change weather patterns in another corner of the globe.

This same sort of deep mutuality applies to our emotions. They weave in and out of one another, like whirlpools in a vast river, or braids in a stream. The entire universe is one immense communication system, carrying information and sending messages. Everybody is implicated in everybody else's business. So attributes such as fear and courage are not simply my personal affair; they have an impact on the universal web of life. They contribute to intense energy fields.

Reflection on experience reveals the contagious character of fear and courage even if we do not recognize the physics behind it. On November 22, 1963, I was a fledgling high school teacher in Portland, Oregon. When I arrived at school that autumn morning, I was assigned supervision of a large study hall set up in the cafeteria. When the announcement that John F. Kennedy had been shot came over the loudspeaker, I was the only staff person with nearly a hundred students. As the magnitude of the tragedy became clear, fear zoomed through the room, passed from student to student, and quickly turned to panic. The students first sat in stunned silence. Then some began to cry quietly. Soon many were sobbing loudly and moving frantically about the room. I stood frozen at the sight, aware that I needed to do something but too inexperienced to know what it was. I will always be grateful to the veteran teacher who realized what might be happening in my study hall and arrived to help me calm the students and ensure their safety. She did this above all by the composure she herself exhibited, as well as by her clear and firm directives that enabled the students to return to their seats and pray with her for the Kennedy family and a grieving nation.

What does it matter if pluck or jitters characterize a group like my study hall students? For one thing, emotions often remain unconscious or unacknowledged. We carry them in masked or displaced forms and may act out of them destructively. Because the response to fear can be fight just as much as flight, it may result in group panic or mass anger. Fear often changes to vengeance or violence. We sum this up by saying that a situation suddenly "turned ugly." Social scientists call it *mob psychology*.

Further, the degree of fear in a society shapes how it regards individual freedoms and personal security. Like a cancer, anxiety can metastasize and eat away at a culture's capacity to reason and act wisely. Depending on how leaders use fear, they may move a community toward constructive action (widespread fear of a nuclear holocaust fueled the determination to eliminate nuclear weapons). Or they can exploit fear to limit freedoms in the name of security, as has happened in many dictatorships and authoritarian regimes. Martin Luther King Jr. used his eloquence to reduce fear and direct the frightened helplessness of many African Americans into nonviolent resistance. He was following the example of Mohandas Gandhi, who did the same as spiritual leader of India. Gandhi saw compassion as a powerful energy stream that could turn the tide of injustice. He defined the enemy not as the other person but as the capacity for violence and exploitation residing in us and in those we define as the other. He regarded love and understanding as the most effective tools for stopping this violence; hatred merely pollutes the energy stream with circulating hate.

Long before either King or Gandhi arrived on the world stage, a spirituality was taking shape among the fourth-century Celtic Christians of Britain and Ireland. Though innocent of quantum physics, Celtic spirituality dovetails well with that contemporary worldview. Drawing on John's gospel and the Bible's Wisdom literature, it reverences creation not as something separating groups of people from one another but as a gift given to all. The light of God dwells at the heart of Creation, and this Light is brighter than all life's terrible sorrows. But lest we romanticize the Celtic tradition, we are told to watch for God's presence in empty, hopeless, and frightening places as well as in beauty and loveliness. As John tells us in his gospel, the Light shines in the darkness, and the darkness has not overcome it. Because this Divine light is woven throughout the physical strands of the cosmos, it

We watch for God's presence in empty, hopeless, and frightening places as well as in beauty and loveliness.

matters greatly how we treat ourselves, the human community, and the body of the universe. We find God by attending closely to life's flow rather than stepping out of it.

The prayers developed in the early centuries of Celtic Christianity flow from daily life. They speak to its rhythms, beauty, and terrors. They round out our circle of belonging, keeping us close to the lights of the sun and moon, and thus to the light of God. A blessing from the *Carmina Gadelica*, a collection of Celtic poems, songs, prayers, and blessings handed down orally, speaks to our own journey of fear and courage.

May the moon of moons
Be coming through thick clouds
On me and on every one
Coming through dark tears.

Courage in the Circles of Marriage, Family, and Work

Most of us do our peace work close to home rather than on the world stage. But recognizing the contagious quality of fear and courage can renew our spirituality of work and relationships. Some years ago, while working at a center for low-income elderly people in downtown Seattle, I took part in crisis intervention training. Because the lives of those we served were so often compromised by homelessness, alcoholism, or mental illness, we had to deal at times with sudden violent outbursts or threats to our own safety or others'. The training deepened my understanding of how emotional energy moves from person to person in a community, and how my own anxiety or composure affects an entire system.

The course suggested forms that love might take in an anxious system such as marriage, family, or work: awareness, attention, presence, and calmness. In the training, we were first taught to be aware of what we ourselves were like when we went to work. For example, were we still processing emotions from previous interactions—an argument with a mate, or frustration with a child who refused to get dressed for school? Next we were to inquire of our work setting, How does this place feel today? This helped us really notice what was going on when we walked into a room. If we did this, we could tell very soon if people were having a good day or a bad one, where the hot spots were, and who needed attention. Being aware enabled us to get to people before a problem flared up.

Then we focused on the quality of our personal presence. Often all it took to reassure a whole group was one person's confident, relaxed bearing. When a situation feels out of control, it spawns fear. But if my voice is calm and I look assured, others can borrow strength from me. Our goal in this training was to learn how to deescalate problems before they had a chance to build and raise the anxiety level of an entire group. One element of that stabilizing was being a good listener and using humor to defuse tension. We learned other ways to intervene in our specific circumstances, but these general guidelines have stayed with me for more than twenty years because they have so often proved helpful in addressing the anxieties found in many systems, from a couple or family in counseling to a meeting of community volunteers.

The social groups that define us (family, workplace, church, synagogue, mosque, nation, universe) pulse with emotional energy. It flows constantly between and among members. Think of any of these systems as a mobile. Touch one part and all the other parts move. Not only people but entire groups can be fearful or fearless. This legacy passes from generation to generation. The descendents of valiant pioneers or survivors of tragedy find the feelings of their elders still pulsing in their bones. Because we are all emotionally connected, our collective healing comes in community. As the Jungian psychologist James Hillman aptly puts it, "There is no way out of the shared environment which is this planet."

The fact that anxiety characterizes systems as well as individuals alerts us to some important aspects of the spirituality of marriage. The Roman Catholic theology of marriage teaches that the couple themselves confer this sacrament on one another, not just on the wedding day but throughout all their years together. This means that each partner becomes grace for the other, mediating the Spirit of God as they comfort and challenge one another. This spiritual vision makes couple interactions, especially communication, a way to have a better marriage and a sacred transaction as well.

How married couples deal with anger usually gets more attention than how they cope with fear. Yet anxiety frequently lurks beneath the anger that stymies communication, shuts down acts of love, and interferes with reconciliation. Each person brings unique fears to a relationship (Will I be forced to do things the way you do? If I name my weaknesses, will I be shamed? Will you still love me if you really get to know me? Are you right about the things you are telling me? Do these faults mean that I'm a bad person?). Since fear makes us vulnerable, it is often transmuted into anger, an emotion that is much easier to express. But anger creates distance between two people, evoking defensiveness and resistance, whereas honestly naming fear opens up communication and makes understanding and forgiveness easier.

Issues surrounding fear and courage influence the quality of family life as well. Many parents wonder how to raise courageous children. A child learns from how he or she (and everyone else in the family circle) is treated. Are family members there for one another when frightening events occur, or are they forced to face them alone? Can they risk bringing truth into their relationships and trust that they can work through conflict when it arises? Family members model courage for one another. A teenager told me: "When my sister went to volunteer with a relief agency, I thought, 'That is so awesome.' I started thinking about becoming a nurse so I could do something just as brave someday." All these experiences show us what it feels like to belong to a circle larger than ourselves, drawing on the encouragement of others to stay confident and resilient.

Living our spirituality at work likewise requires attention to how we manage anxiety. Anxiety is contagious too. What fears do I bring to work? Most of us carry into the workplace concerns about succeeding or failing, being liked and appreciated or the opposite. In the back of our mind, there also lurks some fear of losing a job and being unable to support ourselves. Competition marks most work settings, and it triggers self-doubt and fear surrounding competency.

In *Dancing with Fear*, Paul Foxman describes anxiety as primarily a learned condition, in which family history plays an important role, along with temperament and current stress. Our family history might include anxiety-producing realities such as frequent criticism, alcoholism, marital violence, sexual abuse, or love and approval being given mainly on the basis of achievement. Though everyone experiences anxiety to some degree, Foxman believes that childhood and family background contribute to the personality style of people who are especially prone to anxiety. They are hardworking, perfectionistic, and at pains to please. Conflict is difficult for them; still worse are criticism and rejection. It is important to them to be in control and to try to anticipate the future. Their thinking pattern often includes worrying and negative or judgmental thoughts. They find it hard to let go and relax, even though they would like to. On the positive side, anxiety-prone people also exhibit special gifts: responsibility, excellence, attention to detail, productivity, sensitivity, and a capacity for hard work. The trick is to keep all these traits in balance.

Ignatian spirituality offers a helpful practice for noticing how anxiety is affecting the way we relate in marriage, family, and work. This practice is called an *awareness examen* or examination of consciousness. It requires finding ten or fifteen moments for quiet reflection during the day or at bedtime. The examen is a pause in the midst of a busy schedule, to let God's grace illumine what has been happening. During this time we become aware of undercurrents in our inner life or in our relating that we may have vaguely sensed but did not have a chance to let into full awareness: lingering

The examen is a pause in the midst of a busy schedule, to let God's grace illumine what has been happening.

feelings around a sharp exchange with a child at breakfast, a coworker's response to a comment we made, the pensiveness on a spouse's face as she arrives home from work. The

examen can take many forms and might consist simply
of a prayerful glance over the day as we are about to
fall asleep.

Ignatius saw the examen as a way to listen and
respond to God's action in daily life. In the *Spiritual Exercises*, he describes five aspects of it. We begin with a prayer
of gratitude for the blessings of the day, naming some in
detail. Then we ask the Spirit to give us the insight and freedom to look honestly at our motives and actions, and not to
hide behind deception and excuses. We pay special attention to all of our feelings—anger, fear, shame, envy, anxiety,
jealousy, joy, peace, enthusiasm—especially those we find
intense. Welcoming them without judgment, we let our
prayer flow from what we find. We may ask for strength to
let go of resentment, or for courage to be less afraid of confronting a situation at work. We then ask forgiveness for fail-
ures we regret, and we offer this same forgiveness to others
by releasing hurt and resentment whenever possible. These
steps enable us to look ahead to the next twenty-four hours
with fresh hope and renewed love. We close out the time
with prayers for the next day.

A traditional tale sums up for me the power of the
examen. On an African safari the native bearers, after moving at a swift pace all morning, suddenly refuse to go
another step. "No, they are not tired," says the head bearer,
"nor are they afraid of what looms ahead." "Then why are
you stopping?" asks the explorer. "We have traveled fast,"
replies the head bearer, "and we must now wait for our
souls to catch up."

Transforming Suffering by Sharing Courage

If we listen to the deepest layers of our anxiety, we discover
the universal fear of suffering and pain. We turn to spirituality, hoping for insights on how to cope with these darker
aspects of existence. A student in one of my theology classes
lamented the failure of contemporary spirituality to offer
devotional practices like those that had previously enabled
him to deal with this pain. Educated in Catholic schools,
he was now a prosecuting attorney. He remembered how as
a boy he bravely faced the dentist's chair, fortified by Novo-
cain but also by the realization that he could offer up his
suffering for the souls in purgatory. Now that his theology
no longer supported this practice, he searched for another
way to find meaning in unavoidable pain. He clearly
wanted no part of any spirituality that considered suffering
to be good for you or taught that people ought to bear with
injustices they could remove. He was convinced that Jesus
did not ask his followers to seek the cross for its own sake, or
to remain passive in the face of their own tribulation (or
others'). In fact, the desire to follow Jesus in remedying the
world's sorrow and righting injustice had determined my
student's choice of vocation.

A relational universe, characterized by the intrinsic
communion we have described, makes possible a spiritual
practice of the kind my student sought, one through which
we can both face unavoidable pain and share courage with
others who suffer. The twentieth-century French mystic and
paleontologist Pierre Teilhard de Chardin set a spiritual
context for this kind of prayer. He envisioned an interdependent cosmos in which we are each a part of the vast

river of time. The presence of God pervades not only human life but all of nature as well. Teilhard believed human beings participate in God's ongoing creation and thereby in redemption. In Jesus, God has become involved in the world. The risen Christ constitutes the focal point for all the small things we do each day. Through them we move closer to the reconciliation of all things in Christ, who is the heart of the universe.

Finding God in positive experiences is not so difficult. But in *The Divine Milieu*, Teilhard turns to the slow or swift losses, what he calls the passive diminishments of our lives: natural failing, physical limitation, weakness, disease, and death itself. Our first response to such evils should be to struggle with God against them, to realize that we are to help God lift the chalice of suffering from us and the world. But if we cannot get rid of suffering, we are to find in it the seeds of transformation for ourselves and others, ways in which it might open us to communion with God and the universe.

If we cannot get rid of suffering, we are to find in it the seeds of transformation for ourselves and others.

Building on Teilhard's vision, we can find spiritual practices for sending courage and love to others who are also suffering. Imagine holding in the cup of your hands, like a bird about to be released for flight, the energy you want to send as you unite your suffering with that of others.

Those in pain might be women and children enduring violence in a war-torn country, displaced refugees wandering in search of food and shelter, or the world's mentally ill seeking relief from their torment. You might use a prayer like this: "May your pain be transformed by the Spirit of love who is not far from any of us, but 'in whom we live and move and have our being'" (Acts 17:28).

You may wish to offer this energy of love and courage to others silently, or by simply saying, "I send you love; I send you strength." I often use this mantra when someone I know is undergoing surgery or another medical treatment.

In *The Places That Scare You*, Pema Chödrön describes a Buddhist practice for sharing our heart with others. It is a simple way of remembering our interconnection, and of practicing *tonglen*. This is the Tibetan word for "sending and taking." It consists of a willingness to embrace our own and others' pain and suffering while sending happiness to ourselves and to them. When we encounter pain, we breathe into our heart while acknowledging that others also feel this way. When we experience joy, we breathe and cherish it. Then we wish that anyone who is suffering might be free of it and know this relief and joy, that they may have even the simple pleasure of a sunny day or a fragrant flower. Through such sharing of the heart, we learn to practice compassion and loving-kindness in any time or situation, and the ripples we send out help to heal the planet.

The struggle with fear intensifies as we face physical and psychic pain. Aging raises this specter powerfully, bringing, as it often does, increased disability and proximity to death. Facing these fears or succumbing to depression and despair makes the difference in how we grow old. Jane Thibault, a clinical gerontologist at the University of Louisville Medical School in Kentucky, wanted to find a way to transform the sense of hopelessness and futility that accompany such pain. In 1995, she met with a group of thirteen elderly nuns in an effort to help them deal with their chronic pain. Thibault, who is also a scientist, recognized all the energy the body generates and uses when in pain. She thought it might be possible to convert that energy into the positive spiritual energy of love for others. This conversion involves shifting one's focus from self-in-pain to others-in-need.

Thibault shared her idea with the sisters. It resonated with what they knew of the traditional practice of redemptive suffering, joining one's suffering with that of Jesus for the continuing redemption of the world. Her first visit took place the day after the Oklahoma City bombing, so the nuns dedicated their suffering to the families of its 168 victims. During the year in which Thibault met with the sisters, she noticed dramatic changes. She asked each of them to keep a journal that recorded any psychological or emotional changes they experienced. They met with her monthly in a group, each taking a minute or so to share, if they wished, the nature of their current pain and for whom they would offer it. By the end of the year, they were talking less about their physical symptoms and visiting physicians less. This spiritual practice revived their sense of having a mission. One sister, who had previously isolated herself because of severe arthritic pain, began to visit the library to scan the paper for people and events for whom she could dedicate her personal suffering.

A relational universe offers us spiritual practices that embrace the connections among us in these ways as well as the others we have explored to reduce fear and bolster courage. All these paths foster the spiritual solidarity evoked by Teilhard's hopeful vision for the cosmos. He called love "the most universal, formidable and mysterious of cosmic energies." One day, he believed, we will harness for God these resources of the heart. We will then experience "a second discovery of Fire."

Chapter Ten

The Security of Faith

Spirituality is a *whole* style of living the faith within history through the power of the Spirit.
—MARÍA PILAR AQUINO

WHEN TRAGEDY STRIKES a neighborhood, nation, or global community, we search for direction. We want to know not only how to respond immediately to violence or a natural disaster but how to think, pray, and reposition ourselves in light of it. How can this have happened? Where is God in all of this? Can we ever feel safe again? Is there any way to prevent such occurrences in the future? We yearn for spiritual leadership, for strength and wisdom beyond what we can summon alone.

In such moments, I find myself turning for direction to women and men from the religious traditions who have been an anchor in similar stormy seas. Over time, I have culled from their writings a collection of tenets—a wisdom literature, if you will, that grounds me. These spiritual mentors agree on the foundations of genuine security, and they expand its meaning beyond personal and national safety to include all peoples and the Earth itself. Their words echo the larger truths we know but tend to forget in times of terror or despair. Though they do not always define the specific actions we must take, their vision infuses our response with faith and hope. They furnish spiritual maxims for meditation in harsh as well as tranquil times. These form the sections of this final chapter.

If We Desire True and Lasting Security, We Must Work for Peace and Justice

The Bible offers a vision of security as *shalom*, a community where people live in peace with one another and with all creatures large and small. In such a restored Eden, justice and love are the supreme values. All human beings are recognized as God's Beloved, deserving of an equitable portion of the material goods that make dignity and happiness possible. In such a community, fear no longer rules people's hearts.

The Bible offers a vision of security as shalom, *a community where people live in peace with one another and with all creatures large and small.*

The prophet Hosea portrays this inclusive kind of peace: "I will make for you a covenant on that day with the wild animals, the birds of the air, and the creeping things of the ground; and I will abolish the bow, the sword, and war from the land; and I will make you lie down in safety" (2:18).

On most days, this vision seems beyond us. It requires no less than a total transformation of the world. Such peace flows from the *metanoia* of which Jesus spoke, a complete change of heart, a turning around that sets us straight again. Although the Bible repeatedly tells us not to be afraid, it also points to the way out of fear through love, faithfulness, and mercy, promising that God will complete the work we tenuously begin.

We catch a glimpse of this new creation from time to time, and it burnishes hope. A Jewish rabbi describes how he and his congregation discovered the deeper meaning of their traditional prayer, "*Sim shalom,* grant us peace, your most precious gift, O Eternal Source of peace." Their reflection on this prayer led to an exchange of ideas and resources for creating a world where terrorism would no longer be a compelling choice for so many individuals. The congregation determined to give time and money in support of groups working for peace and organizations dedicated to dialogue between opposing groups. They would educate themselves on the complexity of global issues and find ways to share positive stories of bridge building and compassion.

One of the largest divisions of our time exists among religions themselves. All the major religions speak of peace. As Hindus walk along the Ganges River, they chant "*Shanti, shanti, shanti,*" or "Peace, peace, peace." Jews greet one another with "*Shalom.*" Muslims wish each other "*Salam.*" Christian worship makes frequent use of the word *Pacem.* Yet enmity among the religions themselves often generates hatred and violence.

In *The Still Point: Reflections on Zen and Christian Mysticism*, William Johnston describes a Zen-Christian dialogue he attended in Kyoto in the summer of 1968. Johnston, a Jesuit priest whose work focuses on Eastern and Western meditation, found it an unforgettable week, one in which Christians and Buddhists met in an atmosphere of respect and cordiality. They reached no agreement on philosophical and theological questions; indeed, at that level, their discussions revealed a great divide. Unity among the participants turned instead on shared values: deep meditation, gratitude, nonviolence, and the love of peace. Johnston expressed amazement that such diverse philosophies should produce such similar experiences. But the accord highlighted perennial methods of promoting peace among the religions available not only to leaders but to all members: shared spiritual experiences, working with one another for justice and the environment, education about one another's beliefs and practices, and interreligious conversation.

Seasons of both celebration and tragedy create openings for such sharing. Traveling in India, Tom and I arrived in New Delhi just as Hindus were celebrating Diwali, their annual Festival of Lights. We stopped to buy some beads and then continued on our morning walk. The Hindu shopkeeper from whom we had bought them ran out onto the street and waved us back. He wanted us to bless his family. The joy of the festival brought him and us together in a moment of warmth and benediction.

During Asia's much darker days in 2004, Muslims and Christians, Jews and Buddhists collaborated on disaster relief and projects of rebuilding for victims of a massive tsunami, creating another opportunity for understanding beyond established spiritual borders.

The Peace for Which We Yearn
Begins with Small Actions

In 1979 Mildred Robbins Leet, with her late husband, Glen, founded Trickle Up, a volunteer nonprofit funded by donations. The couple had already spent decades working to bring about social justice and end poverty. Though not a wealthy woman, for twenty-five years Leet gave away fifty dollars at a time to the most destitute among the world's poor to help them launch businesses. The money bought seeds, a sewing machine, a farm animal, fishing rods, frying pans. It supported small ventures of raising chickens in Cameroon, or weaving baskets in Ghana. Skeptics scoffed at such minimal philanthropy, wondering how it could possibly make a difference in the face of large-scale poverty. But Trickle Up launched 115,000 businesses, distributed $3 million, and transformed tens of thousands of lives.

Because of the many modes of instant communication in our era, problems of global proportion deluge us ceaselessly. Sometimes their images energize action, but often the magnitude of the difficulties causes our eyes and mind to glaze over. They generate helplessness, apathy, and despair. However, a parallel truth offsets their negative power: lasting change almost always results from individual or small-group action. Whenever the size of our fear might tempt us to close the blinds and retreat to private concerns, we can envision instead what kind of world we would have if each person did *something*, however limited, to heal its wounds.

This dedication to the importance of small actions is the leitmotif of much spirituality. It characterized the path of the nineteenth-century Carmelite nun Thérèse of Lisieux. In most respects, Thérèse's life was uneventful. It was also short; she died of tuberculosis at twenty-four. But her autobiography, *The Story of a Soul*, published after her death, compellingly describes the holiness possible in ordinary circumstances. Thérèse called this path "the little way." It rooted her so securely in the presence and love of God that it enabled her to carry out everyday actions and endure every small insult. Therese believed that, like a pebble sending ripples through a stream, her way could help change the world.

> *Lasting change almost always results from individual or small-group action.*

Small actions lead to larger results in part because they inspire others. Thérèse's little way informed the spirituality of a powerful twentieth-century woman. Therese was the favorite saint of Dorothy Day, the cofounder of the Catholic Worker Movement. From Thérèse's life, Day learned that every act of love increases the love in the world, and each suffering we endure for the love of God lifts the burden of others' pain. This insight corresponded with Day's conviction that we are mysteriously bound together in the Body of Christ. She translated this spirituality into houses of hospitality that offer food and shelter for the poor. It also sustained her lifelong commitment to nonviolence. Her witness for civil rights and disarmament took her to jail.

Day in turn inspired a generation. Peace activist Daniel Berrigan describes her impact on his own and others' work for justice. In the introduction to Day's autobiography, *The Long Loneliness*, Berrigan says that without her exemplary courage the action of others would have been unthinkable. She jarred their thinking and made the impossible seem probable. She did this, he says, first of all by living as though the truth were really true.

Even earlier than the commitment of Thérèse of Lisieux and Dorothy Day to the little way, the Aztec people of Mexico expressed in story this truth about the salvific power of small efforts. A long time ago a great fire in the forest covered the Earth. When they saw it, all the people and animals started running. Brother Owl, Tecolotl, was also running when he noticed a small bird scurrying back and forth between the fire and the nearest river. He changed course and ran toward the bird.

He recognized the small quetzal bird, Quetzaltototl. He watched as Quetzaltototl ran to and from the river, each time picking up a small drop of water in his beak to throw on the flames. Then Brother Owl yelled at the quetzal bird: "What are you trying to do? You must be crazy if you think you will get any results by that method. Run for your life!"

Quetzaltototl paused for a moment and looked at Brother Owl. Then he replied: "I am doing the best I can with what I have."

Stirred by his words and example, Brother Owl set to work carrying water with Quetzaltototl. Soon other passersby joined them. Now the grandparents of the Aztec people remember that a long time ago a small quetzal bird, an owl, and many people saved the forests covering our Earth by coming together to put out the flames.

Getting to Know Those We Fear Heals Divisions and Builds Understanding

Hatred and division often stem from ignorance. We fear and dislike those who differ from us in race, religion, or socioeconomic status. The alienation and humiliation that arise from this prejudice contribute to violence at every level of society—first oppression, and then violence against the oppression. We have only to think of the student who is bullied in his classroom and how he takes his revenge. In contrast, really listening to one another deepens understanding and engenders tolerance, even if tolerance is sometimes just "putting up with," a kind of reluctant allowing of something to exist.

Really listening to one another deepens understanding and engenders tolerance.

The gospels show us how attentively Jesus listened to those whom society labeled as "other": the Samaritan woman at the well, consumed by a thirst she could not quench; Zacchaeus, the chief tax collector of Jericho, who was too short and dishonest to be taken seriously; the Roman centurion in Capernaum, a powerful soldier whose faith and tender concern for his sick servant moved Jesus deeply. By fully hearing people in this way, Jesus modeled the community of right relationships he wished for us.

My work as a therapist has taught me how attitude toward others changes once we come to really know them, even when we must struggle to open up enough to do so, and though we might end up disagreeing with them. Being invited to listen attentively to a person's story until I really understand it is one of the great gifts my clients have given me. Over the years I have heard the experiences of people at the furthest end of the spectrum from my own religious and political beliefs. In an effort to help clients attend to all the edges of their own experience, I came to see them from ever-new perspectives. This commitment to open and attentive listening resulted in an understanding I might never otherwise have acquired about what it means to belong to a Native American, Buddhist, Hindu, or Muslim faith, or no established faith at all. It taught me that good and thoughtful people hold political views vastly different from my own. The act of listening changed me in many ways. Over time, I felt more connected to people whom I had initially regarded as so different. Though I might never espouse their beliefs, I saw more fully both my own limitations and their strengths and beauty.

In *Turning to One Another: Simple Conversations to Restore Hope to the Future*, Margaret J. Wheatley details her conviction that through simple, honest conversation we can change the world. We especially need to find ways to talk to those we have labeled *the enemy*. Wheatley believes this points a way out of the current cynical, fearful, defensive, anxious state she finds so pervasive among the people she has listened to in many countries. She is convinced that we do not fear people whose story we know; fear separates us, whereas listening brings us closer together. Nothing, she believes, has quite the power to heal that listening does. She describes how the Shona people of Zimbabwe greet one another:

> "Makadii?" (How are you?)
> "Ndiripo Makadiwo." (I am here if you are here.)
> "Ndiripo." (I am here.)

We Will Each Be Safe Only When Every Created Being Is Safe

Nature reassures us with its circles: the roundness of the moon and sun, the cycles of the seasons. But citadels and towers promise a different route to safety from that of circles. In a tower we stand above and apart; we destroy and then retreat. In contrast, circles and webs suggest that we are all in this together. They draw their inspiration from the communion of all beings and an inclusive conception of humanity. Such is the vision of life on our planet received by a medicine man of the Oglala Sioux, Black Elk. Witnessing the Battle of the Big Horn when he was thirteen, and the massacre of his people at Wounded Knee, he was given a vision in his youth that he wished to transmit to all people: "And I saw that the sacred hoop of my people was one of many hoops that made one circle, wide as daylight and as starlight, and in the center grew one mighty flowering tree to shelter all the children of one mother and one father. And I saw that it was holy."

We exist within an intricate web of connections; any thread, any division, can pull apart the tapestry. For native peoples, the phrase *all my relations* describes this kinship. Broader than humanity, it includes all animals, birds, fish, and plants—in fact, all the animate and inanimate forms we can see or imagine. We are expected to embrace the responsibilities that participation in this web brings with it.

A sense of sacred mission similar to Black Elk's marked the call of Martin Luther King Jr. He was pained by the hatred and divisions within the human community. For King, injustice anywhere constituted a threat to justice everywhere. His prophetic role was to try to change an entire nation. He believed we were to create a new and beautiful world, to become the beloved community of peace, justice, and love. To bring about that reality, he turned to Gandhi's principles of nonviolence. Like Gandhi, King found inspiration in Jesus' Sermon on the Mount. Like Jesus, he too met the cross: bombs, death threats, stabbings, stonings, assaults, and in the end assassination.

As a young man, King had no sense that he was called to greatness or the role of prophet; he simply aimed to be a good minister to his congregation. He was only twenty-five at the time of the Montgomery bus boycott in 1955–1956. When first asked to take part in it, he resisted. King was a fallible, often tormented, human being. In *Stride Toward Freedom*, he describes his prayer at one of his low points. It had been a strenuous day, and he went to bed late. His wife Coretta was asleep, and just as he was about to doze off he received an angry, threatening phone call. When he hung up the phone, he could not go to sleep. All his fears came pressing down on him. He got out of bed and walked the floor. He wanted to give up, to get out of the movement. His courage depleted, King turned to God in prayer: "I am at the end of my powers. I have nothing left. I've come to the point where I can't face it alone." In that moment, King says, he knew the Divine presence in a way he had never before experienced it.

King steadfastly embraced nonviolence because he believed that only change built on love prevents us from becoming a mirror image of our oppressors. He sought to convert the hearts of white people, but in a way that would not harden the hearts of black people. The new kingdom of which he dreamed would be long in coming, but King's speeches filled his followers with hope.

Perhaps none of King's words ring as powerfully in our fear-filled times as his last speech in Memphis, delivered the night before he died. In it, he acknowledged that, like the rest of us, he would welcome a long life. But a larger concern filled his soul: the desire to do God's will. God had allowed him to go up to the mountaintop, look over, and glimpse the Promised Land. Though he knew he might not get there with us, he said he was convinced that we as a people would someday reach that land. King's heart held no fear that final night, no worry. He declared that he was happy and at peace. His eyes had seen the glory of God's coming.

Beauty, Humor, and Celebration
Sustain Us for the Long Haul

Followers of Martin Luther King Jr. asked, "How long will it take?" People involved in any great campaign still raise that question. How will we sustain our work for peace over the long haul? For that, we need not only compassion and courage but laughter and beauty as well. Humor affords a glimpse of transcendence, a suggestion that terror, pain, and death do not have the final say. It takes lightly the gap between how things are now and what we believe to be possible. As we manage to find the humor in hard situations, we break open more space for joy and hope. The relief that is brought by laughter bears witness to the reality of redemption.

Many spiritual writers consider humor to be a signal of God's elusive presence in human affairs. The sixteenth-century Spanish mystic Teresa of Avila had a good sense of this. A courageous woman who faced sickness, poverty, investigation by the Spanish Inquisition, and countless obstacles in

Humor affords a glimpse of transcendence, a suggestion that terror, pain, and death do not have the final say.

her reform of the Carmelite order, Teresa never lost perspective. One of her most famous comments stems from the hazards of travel in the customary Castilian mode of the time, the donkey cart. When her cart overturned, dumping her into a muddy river, Teresa complained to God about her travails. She heard a voice within her reply, "This is how I treat my friends." "Yes, my Lord," Teresa retorted, "and that is why you have so few of them."

We also have Thomas More's renowned wit, which he displayed to the very end. More was a highly respected sixteenth-century judge and scholar whom Henry VIII appointed lord chancellor of England. He was arrested and imprisoned in the Tower of London for fifteen months because he could not in conscience take an oath that recognized the annulment of Henry's marriage to Catherine of Aragon, repudiating the authority of the pope. Nor could he support the Acts of Supremacy that made Henry head of the Church of England. Executed in 1535, More quipped with his guard as he made his way up the scaffold: "I pray you, Master Lieutenant, see me safe up, and as for my coming down, let me shift for myself."

Beauty and celebration sustain the long and difficult quest for justice. Just as we cannot stare fixedly at the sun, so we cannot bear unrelenting immersion in the world's problems. Fortunately, there is more to life than tragedy; there are also music, poetry, and other arts of surpassing loveliness. There is nature, which astonishes with sunrises and sunsets, majestic mountains and quiet streams. Beauty fosters resilience and restores energy. Those who struggle for justice also walk in the woods, organize parades, plant trees, tend tulip bulbs, write poems, make love, listen to Mozart, drink wine with good friends, and create art.

A Sufi story points to the reality of God's love as cause for celebration. A certain Sufi determined to follow exactly all the many injunctions of his Islamic faith. In spite of his efforts, however, he never received a vision of God. He registered an appeal to God about this apparent injustice. God replied, "If you want to see me, go to the house where there are song and dance." This astonished the Sufi, for did not the Quran consider these things taboo? Nevertheless, he decided to visit the house of a friend who loved music. As he listened to the songs that were sung, the Sufi received a vision of God. He heard God saying to him: "Taboos make of Me a tyrant—of Me, who am thy lover."

The universe has always been both safe and dangerous, filled with wonder and beset by heartbreak. The courage our hearts desire paradoxically finds assurance in a certain kind of fear, the "fear of the Lord" that the Bible calls the beginning of wisdom. The God evoked by so many biblical images—mother, father, warrior, lover, lion, shelter, fortress, eagle, wind, cloud, and fire—calls forth reverence and awe, dread and attraction. To this God all creation turns expectantly, knowing that our yearning for security will ultimately be answered as God's gift: "For the mountains may depart and the hills be removed, but my steadfast love shall not depart from you, and my covenant of peace shall not be removed, says the Lord, who has compassion on you" (Isa. 54:10).

To this God we pray:

*Creator and Healer, you dwell closer to us than the
air we breathe, yet far surpass all we can know.
We bless you for the stunning beauty of your cosmos,
the gifts you unendingly give.
Forgive us our failure to be grateful and to trust you.
Fill our hearts with your courage, and our minds
with your vision of what we might become.
Free us from fear of the dark unknown spaces where
you give birth to new possibilities.
You are a God of adventure, and you took a great
risk in creating us.
Empower us to become the community of which your
heart dreams.
Amen.*

Notes and Further Reading

Scripture quotations are from the New Revised Standard Version, copyright 1989 by the Division of Christian Education of the National Council of the Churches of Christ in the United States of America; reprinted by permission of the publisher.

Unless otherwise indicated, the prayers, rituals, and exercises throughout the book are my own.

Chapter One: Understanding Fear

The epigraph on fear from Philip Berrigan is in Johann Christoph Arnold, *Seeking Peace: Notes and Conversations Along the Way* (Farmington, Pa.: Plough, 1998), p. 189.

On animal behavior during the Asian tsunami, see Don Oldenburg, "Animals' Reported 'Sixth Sense' Is Explored," *Seattle Times*, Jan. 9, 2005, p. A18.

Gavin de Becker clarifies the positive role of fear in *The Gift of Fear: Survival Signals That Protect Us from Violence* (Boston: Little, Brown, 1997). A national expert on predicting violent behavior, de Becker considers true fear a gift because it is a survival signal that sounds in the presence of danger. De Becker believes we need to distinguish fear from

worry and anxiety, and separate real from imagined danger,
if we want our lives to be less anxious but actually safer.

For clear and stimulating reflections on mind-body connections
and the role of emotion in human life, see the work of neu-
rologist Antonio Damasio: *Descartes' Error: Emotion, Reason, and the Human Brain* (New York: Avon Books, 1994);
*The Feeling of What Happens: Body and Emotion in the
Making of Consciousness* (Orlando: Harcourt Brace, 1999);
and *Looking for Spinoza: Joy, Sorrow and the Feeling Brain*
(Orlando: Harcourt Brace 2003). In *Upheavals of Thought:
The Intelligence of Emotions* (New York: Cambridge University Press, 2001), Martha C. Nussbaum makes a compelling
case for the importance of emotions in our mental and
social lives.

Pema Chödrön discusses compassion and emotion in *The Places
That Scare You: A Guide to Fearlessness in Difficult Times*
(Boston: Shambhala, 2001), p. 33.

Neuroscientists describe what happens with fear. The amygdala,
which is an almond-shaped structure deep in the center of
the brain, sifts information for emotional content and
potential threat. Perceiving a threat, it registers danger, and
this triggers immediate reflexes (we jump or shout). The
amygdala signals the nearby hypothalamus to produce the
hormone called corticotropin-releasing factor, or CRF. This
hormone tells the pituitary and adrenal glands to flood the
bloodstream with adrenaline, norepinephrine, and cortisol.
These are all stress hormones. They close down the body's
nonemergency functions and activate its resources for fight-
ing or fleeing the threat. For more on the neuroscientific
aspects of fear, see Rush W. Dozier, *Fear Itself: The Origin
and Nature of the Powerful Emotion That Shapes Our Lives
and Our World* (New York: St. Martin's Press, 1998).

Patrick J. Howell presents a helpful discussion of the importance
of spirituality in problematic forms of fear in *As Sure as the
Dawn: A Spiritguide Through Times of Darkness* (Lanham,
Md.: Sheed and Ward, 1996).

For the Quran on fear of the Lord, see Scott C. Alexander,
"Fear," in *Encyclopaedia of the Qur'an*, ed. Jane Dammen
McAuliffe, Vol. 2 (Leiden-Boston: Brill, 2002), pp. 194–198.

Chapter Two: Knowing What to Fear

Epigraph from Wilkie Au, "Holistic Discernment," *Presence: An
International Journal of Spiritual Direction*, Feb. 2005,
11(1), 15.

Anne Lamott, *Traveling Mercies: Some Thoughts on Faith* (New
York: Anchor Books, 1999), pp. 79–88.

Ignatius of Loyola: Spiritual Exercises and Selected Works, ed.
George E. Ganss, Classics of Western Spirituality (Mahwah,
N.J.: Paulist Press, 1991). See also Katherine Dyckman,
Mary Garvin, and Elizabeth Liebert, *The Spiritual Exercises
Reclaimed: Uncovering Liberating Possibilities for Women*
(Mahwah, N.J.: Paulist Press, 2001); and David Lonsdale,
Listening to the Music of the Spirit: the Art of Discernment
(Notre Dame, Ind.: Ave Maria Press, 1993).

The James A. Forbes material is from "Deeper Faith: What to
Preach When Uncertainty Is the New Normal. Three
Views," *Leadership*, Winter 2002, *23*(1), 30–33.

Sue Monk Kidd, *The Secret Life of Bees* (New York: Penguin
Books, 2002), p. 211.

Bernard Martin, *John Newton: A Biography* (London: Heine-
mann, 1950), pp. 71–72. See also Jim Haskin, *Amazing
Grace: The Story Behind the Song* (Brookfield, Conn.: Mill-
brook Press, 1992).

Paulette Bauman's comments are from Cara Solomon, "Tent City Offered New Home," *Seattle Times*, Aug. 2, 2004, p. B2.

See Stanley J. Rachman, *Fear and Courage* (2nd ed., New York: Freeman, 1990) for insight into how uncertainty and unpredictability feed fear. His comment on using videotapes with children about to undergo surgery is from Rick Chillot, "What Are You Afraid of? 8 Secrets That Make Fear Disappear," *Prevention*, May 1998, 50(5), 98–104.

David L. Altheide, "Mass Media, Crime, and the Discourse of Fear," *Hedgehog Review: Critical Reflections on Contemporary Culture*, Fall 2003, 5(3), 9–25.

Jim Wickwire and Dorothy Bullitt, *Addicted to Danger: A Memoir* (New York: Pocket Books, 1998), especially pp. xii and 96.

Chapter Three: Living in the Here and Now

Epigraph from Thich Nhat Hanh, *The Miracle of Mindfulness: An Introduction to the Practice of Meditation*, trans. Mobi Ho (Boston: Beacon Press, 1987), p. 12.

See Brother Lawrence, *The Practice of the Presence of God* (Old Tappan, N.J.: Revell, 1958).

Rabbi Rami M. Shapiro describes the Jewish understanding of God as *the Place* in *Wisdom of the Jewish Sages: A Modern Reading of Pirke Avot* (New York: Bell Tower, 1993), pp. vii-xi. He quotes the Hasidic sage Schneur Zalman on p. x.

Pulitzer Prize–winning poet Mary Oliver writes beautifully of the connection of our breath with all of creation. Praying with her poems is a way of deepening this realization. See her *New and Selected Poems* (Boston: Beacon Press, 1992).

David Steindl-Rast, *Gratefulness the Heart of Prayer: An Approach to Life in Fullness* (Mahwah, N.J.: Paulist Press, 1984) is a classic work on gratitude and prayer.

Thich Nhat Hanh uses the example of the magician in *The Miracle of Mindfulness*, p. 14. His discussion of the two sutras, the example of the tree in the storm, and suggestions for focusing on what is right rather than what is wrong are from *Touching Peace: Practicing the Art of Mindful Living*, ed. Arnold Kotler (Berkeley, Calif.: Parallax Press, 1992), pp. 11–18, and pp. 26–27.

Robert J. Wicks offers gentle suggestions for bringing mindfulness to daily concerns in *Riding the Dragon: 10 Lessons for Inner Strength in Challenging Times* (Notre Dame, Ind.: Soren Books, 2003). Sharon D. Welch discusses the relationship between mindfulness and pursuit of peace in *After Empire: The Art and Ethos of Enduring Peace* (Minneapolis: Fortress Press, 2004), pp. 143–158.

The story of the monk and mindfulness is told in Wilkie Au, *Enduring Heart: Spirituality for the Long Haul* (Mahwah, N.J.: Paulist Press, 2000), p. 142.

Chapter Four: Meditation as a Way to Peace

Epigraph from Thomas Merton, *Seeds of Contemplation* (Norfolk, Conn.: New Directions, 1949), p. 22. Merton's autobiography, *The Seven Storey Mountain* (Orlando: Harcourt Brace, 1948) gives a sense of Merton as a young man. His comment on people "shining like the sun" is from his *Conjectures of a Guilty Bystander* (Garden City, N.Y.: Doubleday, 1966), p. 141. For Merton's visit to Polonnaruwa, see *The Asian Journal of Thomas Merton*, ed. Naomi Burton, Patrick Hart, and James Laughlin (New York: New Direction, 1973), pp. 230–236.

My mindfulness meditation on fear is adapted from a method of reflecting on difficulty proposed by Jack Kornfield, in *A*

Path with Heart: A Guide Through the Perils and Promises of Spiritual Life (New York: Bantam Books, 1993), p. 81.

Chödrön, *The Places That Scare You* (2001), p. 50.

Examples of incorporating mindfulness practice into other forms of healing can be found in Jon Kabat-Zinn, *Full Catastrophe Living: Using the Wisdom of Your Body and Mind to Face Stress, Pain, and Illness* (New York: Delta Books, 1990); *Mindfulness and Psychotherapy,* ed. Christopher K. Germer, Ronald D. Siegel, and Paul R. Fulton (New York: Guilford Press, 2005); and *Mindfulness and Acceptance: Expanding the Cognitive-Behavioral Tradition,* ed. Steven C. Hayes, Victoria M. Follette, and Marsha M. Linehan (New York: Guilford Press, 2004).

The Cloud of Unknowing, ed. James Walsh. Classics of Western Spirituality (Mahwah, N.J.: Paulist Press, 1981).

M. Basil Pennington, *Centering Prayer: Renewing an Ancient Christian Prayer Form* (New York: Image Books, 1982), pp. 132–133. Thomas Keating offers a helpful introduction to centering prayer in *Open Mind, Open Heart: The Contemplative Dimension of the Gospel* (New York: Continuum, 1994).

The Asian Journal of Thomas Merton (1973), p. 308.

Chapter Five: Praying When We're Scared

Epigraph from *An Interrupted Life: The Diaries of Etty Hillesum 1941–1943* (New York: Simon & Schuster, 1981), p. 229.

Kay Mills, *This Little Light of Mine: The Life of Fannie Lou Hamer* (New York: Penguin Books, 1993). Quotations are on pp. 18 and 84.

For the perspective of cognitive therapy, see David D. Burns, *Feel-*

ing Good: The New Mood Therapy (rev. ed., New York: Avon Books, 1999); and Dennis Greenberger and Christine A. Pedesky, *Mind over Mood: Change How You Feel by Changing the Way You Think* (New York: Guilford Press, 1995).

Writings from the Philokalia: On Prayer of the Heart (London and Boston: Faber and Faber, 1992). For a fine brief introduction to this method of prayer, see Irma Zaleski, *Living the Jesus Prayer* (New York: Continuum, 1998).

For a discussion of the Islamic perspective on the heart's capacity to contain God, see *Windows on Islam: Muslim Sources on Spirituality and Religious Life*, ed. John Renard (Berkeley: University of California Press, 1998), p. 83.

Lauren Artress, *Walking a Sacred Path: Rediscovering the Labyrinth as a Spiritual Tool* (New York: Riverhead Books, 1995), p. 21.

I am grateful to liturgical dancer Betsey Beckman for all she taught me and my classes about the body and prayer.

Yitzhak Buxbaum includes the tale of the Baal Shem Tov in *Storytelling and Spirituality in Judaism* (Northvale, N.J.: Aronson, 1994), p. 183.

Miriam Greenspan, *Healing Through the Dark Emotions: The Wisdom of Grief, Fear, and Despair* (Boston: Shambhala, 2003), pp. 278–279. Greenspan suggests a number of additional exercises that are helpful in dealing with fear.

On prayer and the imagination, see Kathleen Fischer, *The Inner Rainbow: The Imagination in Christian Life* (Ramsey, N.J.: Paulist Press, 1983).

Chapter Six: Finding Hope in Difficult Times

Epigraph from Cynthia Bourgeault, *Mystical Hope: Trusting in the Mercy of God* (Boston: Cowley, 2001), p. 86.

For the relationship between hope and anxiety, see *Handbook of Hope: Theory, Measures, and Applications,* ed. C. R. Snyder (San Diego: Academic Press, 2000). William F. Lynch made this link some decades ago in his slim classic *Images of Hope: Imagination as Healer of the Hopeless* (New York: New American Library, 1965).

The biblical scholar Walter Brueggemann describes the prophetic role of the imagination in *Hopeful Imagination: Prophetic Voices in Exile* (Philadelphia: Fortress Press, 1986).

On the role of faith after September 11, 2001, see *Walking with God in a Fragile World,* ed. James Langford and Leroy S. Rouner (Lanham, Md.: Rowman and Littlefield, 2003).

George Eliot, *Adam Bede* (New York: New American Library, 1961), pp. 320–321.

Seyyed Hossein Nasr discusses the importance of the Divine Names in *The Heart of Islam: Enduring Values for Humanity* (San Francisco: HarperSanFrancisco, 2002), pp. 4–5; and trust in God's compassion, pp. 205–206. He cites the prayer of the Muslim woman on p. 206. On seeking God as the goal of Islam and on the Sufi practice of remembering the Divine Names, see Frederick M. Denny, *Islam and the Muslim Community* (San Francisco: HarperSanFrancisco, 1987), pp. 72–76 and 87–89. The translations of the Quran are by Nasr, with the exception of verse 10:63, for which I cite Denny's translation. For a clear and readable translation of other selections from the Quran, see Thomas Cleary, *The Essential Koran* (Edison, N.J.: Castle Books, 1998).

Thelma Hall presents an excellent resource for praying with scripture in *Too Deep for Words: Rediscovering Lectio Divina* (Mahwah, N.J.: Paulist Press, 1988).

Chapter Seven: The Love That Casts out Fear

Epigraph from *Sister Thea Bowman, Shooting Star: Selected Writings and Speeches*, ed. Celestine Cepress, (Winona, Minn.: Saint Mary's Press, 1993), p. 19.

The account of the "mad dancers" is from Meyer Levin, *Classic Hassidic Tales* (Northvale, N.J.: Aronson, 1996), p. 86.

Tom Pyszczynski, Sheldon Solomon, and Jeff Greenberg summarize a number of studies showing that high self-esteem reduces anxiety in stressful situations. The importance of self-esteem and its relationship to tolerance is one of the central components of their Terror Management Theory. See their book *In the Wake of 9/11: The Psychology of Terror* (Washington, D.C.: American Psychological Association, 2002), especially chapters three and four, pp. 37–92.

Melissa Gayle West, *If Only I Were a Better Mother* (Walpole, N.H.: Stillpoint, 1992). See also Trudelle Thomas, *Spirituality in the Mother-Zone: Staying Centered, Finding God* (Mahwah, N.J.: Paulist Press, 2005).

This version of the woodcutter's tale is from Heather Forest, *Wisdom Tales from Around the World* (Little Rock, Ark.: August House, 1996), p. 30.

F. Edward Cranz, *Nicholas of Cusa and the Renaissance*, ed. Thomas M. Izbieki and Gerald Christianson (Brookfield, Vt.: Ashgate, 2000), pp. 200–201.

Shelley E. Taylor, *The Tending Instinct: How Nurturing Is Essential for Who We Are and How We Live* (New York: Times Books, 2002), especially chapter six, "Women Befriending," pp. 88–112.

For the positive results women with advanced breast cancer experienced from support groups, see D. Spiegel, J. R. Bloom, H. C. Kraemer, and E. Gottheil, "Effect of Psychosocial

NOTES AND FURTHER READING

Treatment on Survival of Patients with Metastatic Breast Cancer," *Lancet*, 1989, *14*, 888–891.

Judith Herman, *Trauma and Recovery* (New York: Basic Books, 1992), pp. 214ff. In the final chapter on "Commonality," Herman includes the survivors' story from Primo Levi, *Survival in Auschwitz: The Nazi Assault on Humanity*, trans. Stuart Woolf (New York: Collier, 1961), p. 145.

For the neuroscience behind the calming effect of physical contact, see Rush W. Dozier, *Fear Itself: The Origin and Nature of the Powerful Emotion That Shapes Our Lives and Our World* (New York: St. Martin's Press, 1998), p. 137.

The reference to "bunching" in military combat is from William Ian Miller, *The Mystery of Courage* (Cambridge, Mass.: Harvard University Press, 2000), p. 215.

Charles R. Pellegrino describes the mutual tenderness of the dying boy and his father in *Ghosts of Vesuvius: A New Look at the Last Days of Pompeii, How Towers Fall, and Other Strange Connections* (New York: Morrow, 2004), pp. 37–38.

Julian of Norwich, *Showings*, trans. Edmund Colledge and James Walsh (Mahwah, N.J.: Paulist Press, 1978), Long Text, chapter twenty-seven, p. 225.

Chapter Eight: The Core of Courage

Epigraph from Paula Gunn Allen, *The Sacred Hoop: Recovering the Feminine in American Indian Traditions* (Boston: Beacon Press, 1986), p. 13.

Harriet Lerner, *Fear and Other Uninvited Guests: Tackling the Anxiety, Fear, and Shame That Keep Us from Optimal Living and Loving* (New York: HarperCollins, 2004), pp. 26–30.

The role of vulnerability in courage is also a theme in recent psychological writings on women's issues. See Judith V. Jordan, "Valuing Vulnerability: New Definitions of Courage"; and Linda M. Hartling, "Strengthening Resilience in a Risky World: It's All About Relationships," *Work in Progress,* nos. 102 and 103 (Wellesley, Mass.: Stone Center, 2003).

The comment by Mary Alexander is from *Strength in Weakness: Writings by Eighteenth-Century Quaker Women* (Lanham, Md.: Rowman and Littlefield, 2003), p. 129. Emphasis in original.

Paul Tillich, *The Courage to Be* (New Haven: Yale University Press, 1952), pp. 155–190.

Rachel Carson, *Silent Spring* (New York: Houghton Mifflin, 1962). On p. ix Carson addresses her motives for writing the book. See also Linda Lear, *Rachel Carson: Witness for Nature* (New York: Holt, 1997).

On pp. 1–4 of *The Recurring Silent Spring* (New York: Pergamon Press, 1989), H. Patricia Hynes summarizes the opposition to *Silent Spring* as well as the book's impact. The reference to the cartoon about Carson is on p. 1, footnote 1. See also Shirley A. Briggs, "Rachel Carson: Her Vision and Her Legacy," in *Silent Spring Revisited,* ed. Gino J. Marco, Robert M. Hollingworth, and William Durham (Washington, D.C.: American Chemical Society, 1987). Carson's letter to Dorothy Freeman is in Paul Brooks, *The House of Life: Rachel Carson at Work* (Boston: Houghton Mifflin, 1972), pp. 271–272.

The Wisdom of Confucius, ed. and trans. Lin Yutang (New York: Random House, 1938), pp. 20–21.

Kristen Renwick Monroe, *The Hand of Compassion: Portraits of Moral Choice During the Holocaust* (Princeton, N.J.: Princeton University Press, 2004). See especially pp. x-xii and 216–234. The statements from Margot, Otto, and Irene are on pp. 9, 55, and 139.

Empathy also emerges as an important aspect of courage in the research of Selwyn W. Becker and Alice H. Eagly, as reported in "The Heroism of Women and Men," *American Psychologist*, Apr. 2004, 59(3), 163–178.

The stories of individuals coming to the aid of others are from Richard Jerome and others, "Heroes Among Us: When Catastrophe Strikes and Your Life's on the Line, These Are the People You'd Want by Your side," *People Weekly*, Nov. 22, 1999, 52(20), 108ff; and Nick Charles and others, "Beyond the Call: In a Year Defined by Terror, These Everyday People Braved Certain Danger to Save Others from Catastrophe," *People Weekly*, Dec. 10, 2001, 56(24), 88ff.

Quote on the Old Woman is from Allen, *The Sacred Hoop* (1986), p. 11.

For Thomas Aquinas on courage as a cardinal virtue, see *The Cardinal Virtues: Aquinas, Albert and Philip the Chancellor,* trans. R. E. Houser (Toronto: Pontifical Institute of Mediaeval Studies, 2004), pp. 157–205. Augustine's definition of courage is on p. 209. Houser also presents a helpful historical introduction to the doctrine of courage and the other cardinal virtues, from the period of Greek philosophy through the thirteenth century.

Myron Peretz Glazer and Penina Migdal Glazer, *The Whistleblowers: Exposing Corruption in Government and Industry* (New York: Basic Books, 1989). The psychiatrist's statement is on p. 118. See also the Glazers' more recent research in *The Environmental Crusaders: Confronting Disaster and Mobilizing Community* (University Park: Pennsylvania State University Press, 1998).

Chapter Nine: Courage and Fear as Contagious

Epigraph from Martin Buber, *I and Thou*, trans. Ronald Gregor Smith, 2nd ed. (New York: Scribner, 1958), p. 16.

The presentation speech and the complete text of Wangari Maathai's Nobel lecture can be found at Nobelprize.org/peace/laureates/2004.

Joyce Rupp offers a lovely meditation on the new worldview in *The Cosmic Dance: An Invitation to Experience Our Oneness*, illus. Mary Southard (Maryknoll, N.Y.: Orbis Books, 2002).

Helpful resources for exploring Celtic spirituality are J. Philip Newell, *The Book of Creation: An Introduction to Celtic Spirituality* (Mahwah, N.J.: Paulist Press, 1999); John O'Donohue, *Anam Cara: A Book of Celtic Wisdom* (New York: HarperCollins, 1997); and Esther De Waal, *The Celtic Way of Prayer: The Recovery of the Religious Imagination* (New York: Doubleday, 1997).

The prayer is from *Carmina Gadelica*, ed. Alexander Carmichael (Edinburgh: Scottish Academic Press, 1976), III, p. 293.

James Hillman, *The Soul's Code: In Search of Character and Calling* (New York: Random House, 1996), p. 150.

Lerner deals insightfully with anxious systems such as marriage and work in *Fear and Other Uninvited Guests* (2004), pp. 92–116.

Paul Foxman, *Dancing with Fear: Overcoming Anxiety in a World of Stress and Uncertainty* (Northvale, N.J.: Aronson, 1996).

I am indebted to Wilkie Au's discussion of the examen in *The Enduring Heart: Spirituality for the Long Haul* (Mahwah, N.J.: Paulist Press, 2000), pp. 137–140.

Teilhard de Chardin, *The Divine Milieu* (New York: Harper-Collins, 1960), pp. 74–94.

Chödrön, *The Places That Scare You* (2001), pp. 67–68.

Jane Thibault's work is described in Patricia Lefevere, "Transforming the Energy of Pain," *National Catholic Reporter*, Dec. 17, 2004, p. 9a.

The quotations on love and fire are from Teilhard de Chardin, *Building the Earth* (New York: Avon Books, 1969), p. 64; and *Letters to Two Friends 1926–1952*, ed. Ruth Nanda Anshen (New York: New American Library, 1968), p. 81. See also Ursula King, *Spirit of Fire: The Life and Vision of Teilhard de Chardin* (Maryknoll, N.Y.: Orbis Books, 1996).

Chapter Ten: The Security of Faith

Epigraph from María Pilar Aquino, *Our Cry for Life: Feminist Theology from Latin America*, trans. Dinah Livingston (Maryknoll, N.Y.: Orbis Books, 1993), p. 150.

The peace work of the Jewish congregation is described in Leonard Felder, "Prayer as a Rebellion, Part II: How Sacred Words Have Come Alive Since September 11," *Tikkun*, Mar. 2002, *17*(2), 46–47.

William Johnston, *The Still Point: Reflections on Zen and Christian Mysticism* (New York: HarperCollins, 1971), p. xiii.

Ben Dobbin describes the work of Mildred Robbins Leet in "Woman's $50 'Micro Grants' Have Changed Lives of Poor," *Seattle Times*, Oct. 5, 2003, p. A16. See also *Artisans of Peace: Grassroots Peacemaking Among Christian Communities*, ed. Mary Ann Cejka and Thomas Bamat (Maryknoll, N.Y.: Orbis Books, 2003).

The Autobiography of Thérèse of Lisieux (Garden City, N.Y.: Image Books, 1957). A helpful compendium of profiles of heroes and saints in our midst is Robert Ellsberg, *All Saints:*

Daily Reflections on Saints, Prophets, and Witnesses for Our Time (New York: Crossroad, 1997).

Jim Forest, *Love Is the Measure: A Biography of Dorothy Day* (Mahwah, N.J.: Paulist Press, 1986). For the importance Thérèse of Lisieux held in Day's spirituality, see p. 207.

Daniel Berrigan's tribute is in *The Long Loneliness: The Autobiography of Dorothy Day* (San Francisco: HarperSanFrancisco, 1952), pp. xxii–xxiii.

Margaret J. Wheatley, *Turning to One Another: Simple Conversations to Restore Hope to the Future* (San Francisco: Berrett-Koehler, 2002). The Aztec tale is adapted from her version, p. 158. The greeting of the Shona people is on p. 87.

John G. Neihardt, *Black Elk Speaks: Being the Life Story of a Holy Man of the Oglala Sioux* (New York: Pocket Books, 1972), p. 36.

Martin Luther King Jr., *Stride Toward Freedom* (New York: HarperCollins, 1964), p. 134. King's final speech is in *A Testament of Hope: The Essential Writings of Martin Luther King, Jr.,* ed. James Melvin Washington (San Francisco: HarperSanFrancisco, 1991), p. 286. For King's struggle to live out his prophetic call, see Stewart Burns, *To the Mountaintop: Martin Luther King Jr.'s Sacred Mission to Save America, 1955–1968* (San Francisco: HarperSanFrancisco, 2003).

Stephen Clissold, *St. Teresa of Avila* (New York: Seabury, 1982), pp. 234–235. E. Allison Peers gives further examples of Teresa's humor in his preface to *The Life of Teresa of Jesus: The Autobiography of St. Teresa of Avila,* trans. and ed. E. Allison Peers (Garden City, N.J.: Image Books, 1960), pp. 13–25.

The Wisdom and Wit of Blessed Thomas More, ed. T. E. Bridgett
(London: Burns and Oates, 1892), p. 20. See also Louis
L. Martz, *Thomas More: The Search for the Inner Man*
(New Haven, Conn.: Yale University Press, 1990).

For the Sufi tale, see Gurdial Malik, *Divine Dwellers in the Desert*
(Karachi, Pakistan: Royal Book, 1989), p. 26.

Acknowledgments

I owe my deepest thanks to the many people whose support was crucial to the appearance of this book:

The women and men who have come to me for counseling and spiritual direction, and in our time together have taught me about spirituality, fear, and courage;

The Sisters of the Holy Names, for their formation and nurturance of my spiritual life over many years;

Paul Fitterer, Katherine Dyckman, Karen Barta, Donna Orange, D'vorah Kost, and Shanta Iyer, for countless helpful conversations;

My counseling colleagues, Phil Abrego, Eric Peterson, Judy Harris, Carolyn Corker-Free, and Rita Breshnahan, for group consultations laced with healing laughter;

Joan Saalfeld, Pat Steffes, Jane Kopas, Edwin Beers, Joan O'Neill, Dana Greene, and Irene Fischer-Davidson, for their encouragement and perceptive reading of my work;

My editor, Julianna Gustafson, whose counsel, warmth, and enthusiasm nurtured this project from its inception;

My husband, Tom Hart, who in innumerable ways made this book so much better than it would otherwise have been.

The Author

K athleen Fischer has been a teacher, counselor, and spiritual director in Seattle, Washington, for more than twenty years. She received her Ph.D. from the Graduate Theological Union in Berkeley, California, and an M.S.W. from the University of Washington. She is the author of numerous articles and books, including the award-winning books *Transforming Fire, Autumn Gospel,* and *Women at the Well.*